A VIEW FROM A BELFAST WINDOW

By the same author
A Journey through my Life. Merlin 1989

A VIEW FROM A BELFAST WINDOW

Ernest Morrison

JANUS PUBLISHING COMPANY
London, England

First published in Great Britain 1993 by
Janus Publishing Company

Copyright © Ernest Morrison 1993
British Library Cataloguing-in-Publication Data.
A catalogue record for this book is available from the British
Library.

ISBN 1 85756 091 4

Cover design David Murphy

Printed and bound in England by
Antony Rowe Ltd, Chippenham, Wiltshire

CONTENTS

A View from a Belfast Window   1
The Herring Woman   4
Mental Scars   6
The Lost Message   7
The Rose   9
Old Mutt   10
Stuart, Resting in Peace   13
Roselawn   22
The Traveller   23
The Prodigal   24
Shoreleave   25
The Call   26
I Don't Want to Go to Africa   28
Paddy in Persia   30
Father   31
In My Father's Footsteps   33
Old Shoes   36
My Mother's Hands   38
Brother   41
Aging   42
Man on a Mountain   44
The Street   45
Orchestral Rains   46
Thoughts in the Firelight   48
Silence   54
Screams of Absence   58
Father and Daughter   64
Belfast, City of my People   66
Death of Reason   69
Divers in Saudi   70
Simple Prayer   71
The Diver   73
The Old Diver   74
Voice of the Masses   76
From Dunglow to the Desert   78

v

The Great Deterrent   79
Five Sentence Existence of Man   80
As I am Judged   81
Harsh Judgement   82
The Drinker   83
Paranoid Alcoholism   85
The Migrant Mind   90
Little Leaf   92
Paddy's Destiny   93
Hope   95
Lord, to be a Child Again   97
The Giant Oak   100
Car Wreck   101
Old Rope   102
Low Spirits   103
Contradiction   104
Prayer of the Working Man   105
1969 . . .   107
Tir Na Nog   110
The Launching   112
The Hunchback   113
A Vapor Trail   115
The Escapist   116
Tainted Angel   117
Grim Harvest   120
Silence of the Stars   122
Wrath of Odin   124
Once   127
Feeling   128
Away   130
Song of Solitude   131
Seasons   132
What's Left . . . Is . . .   133
Bereaved   134
Yesterday's Friend   136
Blue Eyes   137
My Island   139
Lust by Candlelight   141
Look Back Sometime   142
Gathering Dusk   145

Beside Myself   146
Cold Picture   148
Death of an Author   149
The Iceman   151
Soul to Soul   153
The Ee-Ven-Gel-Est   155
The Observer   157
Battle Weary   158
Four Words in Prayer   160
Wages of Terror   161
The Taker   162
A Shipyard Yarn   167
The Misfit   169
Virus from the Stars   171
Saint or Savage   173
Terrorist   175
The Order of the Shadows   176
Angel or Insect?   179
Circular Road   181

A View from a Belfast Window

Stay back from the window children,
Can't you hear the shooting?
On the streets are people dying,
In the town the crowds are looting.

But Mama there's a soldier there,
He's wounded and he's bleeding,
And no one goes to help him Ma,
I hear the soldier pleading.

Get back from the window child,
There's nothing you can do,
Just pray the young man might survive,
And thank God it isn't you.

But he's so young and so alone,
He's frightened and he's dying,
Mama come and listen please,
I hear the soldier crying.

Someone's running to him now,
Two men, one young one older,
And both are reaching out their arms,
Christ Ma, they shot the soldier!

Oh Mama, why'd he have to die?
Someone so young as he,
Why is this land so cruel Ma?
Why can't the young be free?

Ah child, I have no answers now,
Your questions break my heart,
But ever since I was a lass,
This land's been torn apart.

I've seen this death, of young and old,
I've heard the victory claims,
But when the gunsmoke clears away,
There's only dead and maimed.

But Mama, do they have to kill?
Please tell me, where's the reason?
I'm trying hard to understand,
How death can be so pleasin'.

Does it make much sense Ma?
A better life for one another,
To plant a bomb, or raise a gun,
To massacre your brother.

And when the people bleed and die,
What wonders are achieved?
And what is better in this world,
For killer or bereaved?

Ah child, please stop, please ask no more,
I'm just as lost as you,
This old world waits for God to act,
There's nothing we can do.

Well Ma, it seems so hopeless then,
I don't think I can take it,
I watched that poor boy coldly killed,
Whilst I prayed to God he'd make it.

Does God ever really listen Ma?
Does Ireland get a mention?
Or is Heaven much too busy Ma?
To pay the least attention.

They're back there at the soldier Ma,
They've stripped him of his clothing,
They've robbed his body, kicked his face,
They fill my soul with loathing.

2

If I'd a gun this moment Ma,
I'd kill those heartless bastards,
I'd take my gun and shoot each one,
Who cares what happens after.

Don't you see my foolish child,
Twas hatred killed the soldier,
You've witnessed death, you feel their hate,
And suddenly you're older.

Awhile ago you ask me why,
These people had to kill,
Now the hatred has a hold on you,
You'd do it with a will.

And if you killed the killers child,
This world would be no better,
And you a link within the chain,
Of death going on for ever.

That window's just a glimpse of life,
You've looked, now learn the lesson,
Will you become so evil too,
Or let it be a blessin'?

To kill the killers, little one,
Would send your soul to Hell,
Someday they'll face the wrath of God,
Shall you be judged as well?

The soldier's dead, the killers gone,
This sad old world's not changed,
No blow for freedom's been achieved,
And history still remains.

So, don't go out to find a gun,
But arm yourself with prayers,
Ask God to tell the soldier's soul,
Of the little Irish boy, who cares.

The Herring Woman

Remember the Herring woman?
Bespeckled and scaled,
Who pushed her old cart from the markets.

Into the cobblestoned streets where we lived,
She came screaming her wares, like a harlot.

'Herns my lovelies, fresh from the sea,
Herns fresh caught today,'

Fishscales to the elbows, on her face in her hair,
She would swat the bluebottles away.

'Herns, fresh herns, for a shillin' a pound,
A wee morsel for yer man comin' home,
Grant him he's wish, put a fish on he's dish,
Sure he might take ye out to the "Drome".'

Echoes of yesteryear, faces and places,
Feelings that won't go away,
The old Herring woman,
The Hobbyhorse man,
The Lamplighter, who'd end the day's play.

The clatter of hooves,
The snow on the roofs,
The tracks left by Harkness's carts,
Old neighbours of ours, standing talking for hours,
Winters warmed, by the glow of their hearts.

Now, the Nuclear age,
Nations set to engage,
In destruction, on Earth and in Space,
I look back with a sigh,
And in my mind's eye,
See,
The scaly old Herring dear's face.

Mental Scars

Dark was that room, where he was small,
Too little and scared to shout or call,
Afraid to make a sound at all,
As the shadows closed around him.

He'll remember, remember, forever more,
Those sounds that came through the bedroom floor,
As his battling parents would scream and roar,
Whilst the evil darkness bound him.

Crouched in the corner, fingers in teeth,
Curled up tight, little shivering leaf,
Small heart pounding with pain and grief,
Until the morning found him.

The Lost Message

He was stooping down,
Drawing in the dust with His finger,
His hair veiled the side of His face,
So that only an ear and part of His beard were visible.

He was writing, with a finger in the sand,
The hem of His garment was filthy,
His feet and sandals stained with a mixture of mud and sewage
through which He and His followers had tramped,
In town after town after town.

He was weary, needing rest,
Needing respite from the endless crowds with their ailments and
diseases, their suspicious doubts and accusations, their blind
and their paraplegic.

This mob were growing impatient,
Demanding His Judgement, His condemnation,
And the stoning of the poor adulterous creature they'd thrust
before Him, seeking, through her to entrap Him.

But He remained stooped, silent, unperturbed,
Writing in the dust.

Then, He rose and said,
'Let he among you, that is without sin, cast the first stone.'

He stooped once again, continued writing in the dirt, with His
    finger.

The angry murmurs subsided,
The curses fell away,
The damning tongues were still,
And stones clenched in eager fingers, dropped to the ground,
    and lay inanimate, unbloodied.

Quietly, one at a time the crowd dispersed.
The trembling woman stood alone and fearful.

Rising, sweeping back His hair He asked,
'Where are those who condemn you woman?'
'No one has condemned me Master.'
'Nor shall I condemn you, go thy way' He said, 'and sin no
    more.'

These words he spoke,
Her soul and her life were saved,
The mob's own guilt turned against them,
This we know.

But my ears tingle,
My eyes yet strain,
My heart aches to know,
My mind screams for enlightenment,

Please, Lord, Lord,

What did we miss,
What should we have seen?

Lord?

What message trampled on by many feet,
Obliterated by man, goat, and oxen,
And covered forever by the dust of the street,
Please, Lord, what was written, there, in the sand?

The Rose

Love the rose,
That lives a season,
That blossoms, blooms,
And dies for reason.

'Time' the master,
Of the rose,
Dictates how long,
She blooms and grows.

'Time' will tell her,
Summer's gone,
And tragic Autumn,
Comes along.

A petal falls,
And blows away,
Another falls,
Another day.

And though the sweet rose,
Fades and dies,
Her beauty lives,
Within my eyes.

I can forgive,
The loss of grace,
And seasons change,
Her lovely face.

Not so.
The careless, graceless dunce,
Who sheds her petals,
All at once.

Old Mutt

Scraggy, mud-caked coat,
Tail, tucked over essentials and curled between hind legs,
For slim protection of procreation parts,
Once proudly displayed.

Legs so weary,
Those tender worn paws scrape ground, as he moves,
slopingly along.

No more,
The disdainful prancing trot, or high tail strut,
Now, just the 'head low between shoulders' skulk.

He slinks along, desiring only, blessed inconspicuousness,
Hoping in vain, to survive the day, without a kick,
or a cuff,
A well hurled stone,
Or the wrong end of some pedigree pooch master's stick.

I see you old dog, mucus around your half-blind eyes,
Snot oozing from your nostrils,
Crudded froth at your grey muzzle,
Brown, broken, aching teeth,
And ancient fleas on your bent and bony back.

No master's voice for you,
No gentle head-patting hands, or guiding whistle,
No doggie bowl, your name ostentatiously, emblazoned on its
    side,
Contents regularly replenished,
The rewards of spurious human affection.

What sad circumstance, brought you to destitution, old mutt?
Did cuddly puppyhood desert you?
Did your lack of etiquette, finally betray you?
One damp smelly spot too many, on copiously stained
expensive carpet?
Earning you the order of 'the boot?'

So you blew it,
Well, welcome to the world old mutt.

And how is the hungry hobo life?
Hunted and harassed,
Reeking and rejected,
Plundering and pilfering,
A new wound gained for every morsel,
Eating repulsive filth and glad of it.

Were you young once?
Happy?
Softly petted and well housed,
Ever a small boy's friend?

Well look at you now,
An abomination to your canine god.

Seeking some sheltered nook, to lay your mangy head,
Slinking off into the drizzling rain,
Dreaming of better days.
Longing for the courage to end your misery,
Under the wheels of some thundering juggernaut,
Wishing only to cease your pointless existence,
To succumb peacefully, in the sweet comforting arms,
Of blissful death.

There ought to be a doggie heaven, for such as you, old pal,
Crawl away now, whimper off into the shadows,
Look not to me for comfort, or wise counsel,
I fare little better than you, in this life, old comrade.

I hope you find your plush meadow, old dog,
Where you can laze your last days, in summer sun,
By a running stream,
To cleanse your lonely degradation,
Crawl away now, crawl away and hide,
I have seen you old mutt,
I know you well.

Stuart, Resting in Peace

I never thought of myself as ephemeral,
Short lived,
Never thought of it at all,
Really.

You were at pains to teach me,
Things,
Life,
Rights and wrongs,
The wisdoms.

You struggled to teach,
I struggled to learn,
Wanted to be,
All that you wished me to be,
For your sake.

For myself,
It never really mattered,
This life,
Its laws,
Rules and regulations.

I was always . . .
Apart!
You see,
Being me,
In the world,
Well, in my world anyway,
Without the rules.

No one's fault.

I was just, all bent out of shape,
Living,
It was . . . uncomfortable,
Heavy.

That world in which you all seemed to cope so well,
For me it was,
Oppressive,
Threatening,
Insecure.

Insecurity dwelt within me,
Present,
Always,
Like a heartbeat.

Not something anyone put there,
Just part of my life,
Like a hand, or an eye.

I wish,
I hadn't hurt you,
Doing what I did,
Suicide!

Don't blame yourselves.

It was me,
The way I was,
It was my solution, you see,
To ease my discomfort,
I 'side-stepped',
Decided to pass, on life,
I chose to forfeit.

There is, a price to pay,
Of course,
A high price,
Being without you.

But I am learning now,
Be assured,
We shall overcome that,
With time.

Suicide,
Seemed like the answer, back then.

Oh, I needed all the tools,
The anger,
The frustration,
I was building it you see,
Building the foundation,
For my final move.

I used everything there was to use,
You, all of you,
Myself, how I'd lived,
Hurting myself, hurting you.

All bricks in the wall, you see,
Fuel for the fire.

I needed to arouse my wrath,
And while I vented my rage,
Fed the anger,
Fanned the flames and prepared myself,
All the while I was loving you,
Yes, I know I said things,
Wrote!
Angry, you see,
But I never blamed you,
Not in my heart,
Never hated you,
Not any of you,
My parents, my family?
I loved you.

But I had no love for life,
None at all,
None!

The note,
The accusations,
They were just my springboard,
My release,
The conjuring up of reasons,
Something to act upon,
I wanted out!

Loved you all,
Being your son,
Your brother,
Loved you truthfully,
But the desire to forfeit,
Was overwhelming.

Selfish?
Yes, I suppose,
But it was so strong, you see,
My disquiet,
My discontent,
My awful discomfort.

I belonged to you,
Great, no problem,
But could never feel, I belonged to life,
That!
Was a problem!

I denied you your rights,
I know that,
I'm sorry, truly sorry,
Had you known, you would have helped me,
But I didn't want you to convince me,
Or talk me out of it.

It was such a strain,
All of it,
I didn't want it.

The rewards offered by life,
Never justified the effort required,
Not to my mind.

Try to understand,
I was unhappy,
You didn't make me unhappy,
I WAS unhappy, period!

The world held no appeal,
I wouldn't have been any good at it,
Already at fifteen years old,
I knew I was making a hash of it,
Knew it would get worse,
Me getting it wrong,
Doing things,
Mistakes,
Failing, floundering,
Making your lives hard.

Hurting you and hurting myself,
Never wanting to,
Just inevitable,
I didn't want that,
Chose to go instead.

Please,
Don't feel bad,
Don't let sadness,
Regrets,
Misplaced guilt,
Destroy you.

You were not responsible,
My choice,
No one else's,

Absolutely my choice,
To go.

I felt within myself,
An absence.

What I mean is,
Sometimes living seemed,
Like an exercise,
In Surrealism,
Abstraction.

I felt I was there,
And yet not there,
A vague temporariness,
I felt sometimes,
As though I stood,
Only on the threshold,
Of existence,
Only on the threshold.

I never had a tight rein on life,
I was on the borders,
With no real desire to venture in.

I ventured out!
I wished it that way.

I'm so sorry I hurt you,
All of you,
You didn't deserve that,
I loved you,
I love you.

Death,
Is a door,
We never really lose each other,
Never!

I, am in your hearts,
You are in mine.

And it is the scheme of things,
That we shall be together again,
Where joy and happiness reign supreme.

Don't ever doubt that.

Didn't Jesus say,

'Come unto me,
All ye who are heavily burdened,
And I shall give thee rest'?

Mum,
Dad,

Jesus took my burden.

Please, don't despair,
I am happier now,
Wiser,
Better informed,
I see clearly now,
Things you tried to teach,
Which I failed, or didn't wish to learn.

I could never have gotten it right,
Not in that life.

Don't grieve,
Grieving, you will only make me pay,
For what I did.

Forgive me,
I wish I hadn't hurt you, so deeply,
But,
I wanted out!

I am happier now,
Unburdened,
Enlightened,
I miss you,
But time will overcome that.

I am happier,
Be happy for me,
I know I hurt you,
Dreadfully,
But please,
Don't hurt yourselves, or me now,
By blaming yourselves.

It was all so far,
Beyond your control.

Some people would fly in the face of God,
Blame God for 'letting it happen'
But it was my suicide, my act!

God permitted me,
One last sin,
Because,
God is Mercy,
And,
I will sin no more.

In Spirit and soul,
I, am your son,
In any life.

You are my Mum and Dad,
My brother and sister.

And I am still Stuart,
But,
A happier, fuller Stuart.

Live your lives for me,
Bless God.
He saved me from myself.

And He didn't do it,
Nor was it meant to be,
At the cost of your misery.

Have faith!
Be happy,
Live for each other,
And love me as I love you.

I know,
You won't forget me,
Nor I you,
Ever!

Ours,
Is eternity,
Together!
Secured in the love of God.

Always remember,

Despite everything,
Words, deeds and pain.

I am your son,
Your brother.

And as true as my soul rests,
In the cup of God's gentle Hands,

I will love you always,
Stuart.

Roselawn

I stood upon a cold hill,
Where death lay young, and innocent,
At my feet.

Each thought, I studied, in those moments of solitude,
As a botanist studies a single flower,
But this small flower,
Was forever closed,
And no warm Spring shall come to rescue.

What a wound to our hearts,
Is this small grave,

I kicked at a stone,
And cursed at reason.

What reason,
What learning,
For what painful sad purpose,
Must dead youth lie still in eternity,
On this cold and wind-pierced hill?

Where are the labourers,
Who shall till this soil,
For the harvest of my understanding?

The Traveller

Lying in the cradle of my left arm,
Your head on my shoulder,
Your fingers playing in the hairs on my chest.

You are at peace,
Sexually satisfied,
Physically contented,
Ready for sleep.

Your soft breath becomes shallow and even,
Your fingers cease and are still,
You drift into gentle slumber,
I know the slowing of your heartbeat,
Shan't stir,
Lest I wake you.

Through all the long, quiet, painful night,
I am moving, moving, moving,
Over dust-blown plains,
Snow-capped mountains,
Deep green forests,
And moonlit seas,

Immeasurable distances,
Away from you.

The Prodigal

A Prodigal rover, no four leaf clover,
One life best over before it's begun,
One wandering Paddy, a 'drunk?' and a Daddy,
But sure what chance had he?
Just a prodigal son.

One lonely stranger, a soul deep in danger,
Who dreams of the 'Manger' and the 'Cross' of his Lord,
One sick at heart, one so torn apart,
One wrong from the start, walks alone midst the hordes.

One with regrets, one who never forgets,
One who gives all he gets, knows greed never pays,
One far away, toils in silence each day,
One who's destined to pay, for the 'sins' of his ways.

One who believed, one who must grieve,
One who always must leave, though he's wishful to stay,
One who built 'Hope' whilst he struggled to cope,
One whom 'Utopia' possessed and betrayed.

Now one who must choose, every way, he must lose,
Who would stand in these shoes?
On these last of my days.

Shoreleave

Be still, my tender love, lie soft and still,
Let these strong arms enfold you, while they may,
In the east there comes the creeping light of day,
And soon I must arise and sail away,

Be still, a little while my love, be still,
The dawn approaches with its evil chill,
And once again I must, against my will,
Depart your cosy breast, far, far, to stray.

Although I curse and rant and rave and shout,
The morning tide comes in to take me out,
And though I wish and plead and ache and pray,
Tides must come in, as I must go out,

Go out,
And wander oceans, far away.

The Call

In the sweat-soaked semi-delirium,
Of my shallow sleep,

I see it again.

Over the sun-scorched dust-blown dusky plain,
A black,
Disembodied hand,

Gesticulates,

A lean finger crooks and curls,
Commanding me to come.

I know this fearful vision,
It haunts my sleep.

A precognitive dream.

I twist and turn,
Seek a sanctuary,

But the mirror of my fate persists,
In the reflection of my future.

There shall be no excuse,
No concealing of myself,
No side-stepping of the inevitable.

I must rise and go,
No choice, no luxury of choosing.

The cruel continent calls.

I must summon all my courage,
And fly face forward to fate.

But I damn this dream,
This evil dream,

Through which,

Africa beckons.

I Don't Want to Go to Africa

It's happened again,
The dream!

In my sleep,
The famine-crazed hordes,
Camp on my chest,
And whisper their suffering,
Against the dam of my subconscious.

In that damned dream,
I flee their distended bellies.
Turn from a child's dying gaze.
And rip my flesh to shreds,
In anguish.

Oh God, whose suffering is this?
Is it really theirs,
Or everyman's?

Is it mine?
Am I to be consumed,
In the roaring furnace flames,
Of my own helpless conscience?

Tell me Lord,
How can they who suffer, accept?

Whilst we who don't,
Cannot!

And what hand did I play,
In dealing out their destiny,
Of destruction,
That they claim my very sleep?

Why, why,
Does it smite me so?

These hungry generations,
Feast upon my heart,
And trample my sanity,
Into African soil.

Sleeping,
Or waking.

I don't want to go to Africa.

But Africa, beckons.

Paddy in Persia

Yes there are palm trees,
And Oases so rare,
Desert rose is occasionally found,
Here and there.

Persian waters are warm,
And the sun always shines,
Yet if joy can be found here,
My sad heart declines.
There is strength in these hands,
My arms are like bedrock,
But my soft Irish heart,
Is pining for Shamrock.

Father

This is a rose,
From my garden, father.
I brought it here, for you.

The possession of gardens,
Or flowers,
Or trees,
Was something you never knew.

Now, here you lie,
In this small,
Plot of land,
And this sweet rose you cannot see.

Of all in this world,
You denied to yourself,
Please,
Accept this small wonder, from me.

Your Universe,
Was East Belfast,
From Beechfield Street, to the 'Yard'.

Your rewards were small,
Your joys were few,
Your whole life,
Was intolerably hard.

I was a child,
You a stern old man,
With a temper that taught me fear.

Yet can you believe,
All these years,
I still grieve,
And I've come to your grave,
To be near.

You carried your load,
To the end of the road,
And your 'road' ended here,
At this grave.

With Beechfield Street gone,
And your working days done,
Life released you, a work-worn old slave.

So this is a rose,
From my garden, father,
It shines beautifully white, in the sun.

And I brought it,
To beg for your pardon, father,
And,
To thank you for all that you've done.

In my Father's Footsteps

Fifty years in the shipyard,
1914 to '64,
Until that day he cycled his bike,
From the shipyard forevermore.

Apprenticed there, to the plating,
A Plater all his days,
But those dexterous fingers could ply such skills,
In so many different ways.

He could take an ugly old piece of wood,
And carve there an objet d'art,
Oh the magic he wielded over chisel and plane,
Man and tools sculpted pride in my heart.

He was ever the nose to the grindstone type,
Hard at work and more honest than most,
How the memories dwell, in the caves of my mind,
I am haunted by my father's ghost.

Was it worth it, old man, half a century gone,
And with no worldly goods to impress?
No material gain for your years and your pain,
Start with little, to finish with less.

Ah sure, all that you ask was the brew in your glass,
A few evenings down at the bar,
No holidays, travel, nothing outside the 'Yard'
You were destined to never go far.

Had you aspired to be greater than this,
You may have achieved something brave,
But content with your lot, all that you hadn't got,
You just cycled from shipyard to grave.

Well, my father, I won't be held down as you were,
I won't be a slave to the wage,
I shall fulfill my duty, till my children have grown,
Then I'll storm this old world in a rage.

Your gift with the tools that long caused me to gape,
In awe of your wonderous skills,
Your mastery so long I wanted to ape,
But I've seen how the working life kills.

It killed you in spirit, it stole your whole life,
It left you to die, lost in pain,
I have seen what it did, and I've learned of it now,
And I don't need the lesson again.

You had your tools and your ships and your wood,
Did they serve you, or did you serve them?
For all that you'd earned, when your candle was burned,
Was a box and a whispered Amen.

So I never followed your footsteps, father,
I possess neither plumb-line nor plane,
And I've never stood in the shipyard father,
I'm a child of the wind and the rain.

There's one thing I do, which may have pleased you,
Instead of your chisels and nails,
I sit in the night, with a heart that takes flight,
And I travel the written words trails.

You might understand I'm a writer, old man,
And I hammer this page with my pen,
I carve every line, with the edge of my mind,
As it rides on some mystical plane.

This pen is the wind, and words are the sails,
And the ship I build shapes like a book,
And at moments like this, when your old face I miss,
I so wish you could just take a look.

No I'm no shipbuilder down at Harland and Wolf,
And I'm hopeless at working with wood,
I have never conformed to the call of the 'Horn'
Though many folks thought that I should.

But father, you know, every man has to grow,
To fit into the world best he can,
And I am what I am, and accept what I am,
I just hope that you'd understand.

Now I've roamed this old globe, and I've seen many things,
I've known danger, and lone years so hard,
But I'll gamble my life, in some land torn with strife,
Before dwindling it dry, at the 'Yard'.

I'll be home this Christmas, of '88.
Back home to old Belfast.
And I'll come to stand at your feet for a while,
At that spot where you're resting at last.

Would you know me, father if we could meet,
Would you gasp at the change in my face?
Where this war-torn Earth has given birth,
To ravages time won't erase.

But then father, my world is not your world,
And our lives in no way compare,
Yet still you should know, that it saddens me so,
To return home, and you're never there.

Those are footsteps I'm destined to follow father,
Those last faltering footsteps you made,
Before you lay down, and we all gathered round,
To lay you at peace in the shade.

I suppose then, regardless of what route we choose,
Life's journey ends, always the same,
I've tried to make contrast 'twixt your life and mine,
But sure all life returns, whence it came.

Old Shoes

Only a pair of old shoes,
Dust-coated, ragged laces
Two ancient bits of sometime past,
At rest in two small spaces.

Can't force myself to throw them out,
To burn them or discard them,
Old shoes that walked beside me once,
That's how I still regard them.

These two old shoes beside my bike,
Strong hands that held me steady,
Warm voice that whispered in my ear,
'I'll hold you till you're ready'.

Old shoes that tapped a melody,
Which set our small hearts ringing,
A voice that yet sounds in my head,
Irish eyes, he's singing.

Old shoes that strode beside my Mum,
Her eyes then filled with laughter,
And oft times when her tears were shed,
Strong arms that held her after.

Old shoes with cardboard insoles cut,
Protection from the weather,
Though full of holes the old man rose,
Some shine upon that leather.

The years roll on, their gleam has gone,
As are the feet that wore them,
But how the years go tumbling back,
Each time I stand before them.

Old shoes with leather uppers scuffed,
And heels beyond redemption,
But every time I glance their way,
They capture my attention.

My sister sitting on his knee,
Enchanted by a story,
His old face lightened with a smile,
Brow cracked with toil and worry.

Old shoes that walked to Harland's yard,
Or cycled many winters,
Old hands all calloused scarred and worn,
Old heart like glowing embers.

Old shoes that walked my childhood days,
So still now, on this floor,
Old face, old feet, my memories tread,
Old man, I miss you sore.

My Mother's Hands

It's the hands I think of, often,
Oh, I see your face quite clearly,
Here, in my mind's eye,
The crinkled skin, and silver hair,
The dark eyes, still dancing with life at eighty.
But often, I think of the hands.

Weathered skin, ravaged by toil and climate,
Once supple strong and tender,
A mother's hands, which held me,
As an infant, clothed me, fed me,
Kept me dry and warm and safe,
Those hands that sheltered and soothed me,
While I cried and yapped,
Demanding evermore, of everything,
Oblivious of any understanding,
That your poor heart ached with the pain,
Of having no more, of anything, to give.

We never really knew hunger, us kids,
But you did. You, knew all their was to know,
Of hunger and deprivation,
And of working those hands, to exhausted frozen immobility.
So that we, might have all that we needed,
Whilst you longed to give us all that we demanded,
Beyond all possibility.

You ever saw to it, that we had enough,
But in our childhood ignorance,
Nothing, was, ever enough.

Those hands, which, by their merest touch,
Could inexplicably, ease our pains,
Could magically stop our tears,
And, by their comforting nearness,
Alleviate childish fears of shadows, uncertainties,
The insecurities of this life.

Those hands, that washed and scrubbed our bodies,
Cleansed our clothes, our home, our lives,
Shopped for, carried and cooked, on and on,
And on and on. . .
How often, did any of us ever say? 'Thanks Mum'
Or 'Take it easy, rest now, you've earned it.'

No. We were growing, sprawling brawling boys and girls,
Wrapped up white and tight, in our own selfish existence,
And adolescent questions,
'Why isn't life wonderful?'
'Why isn't Mother the perfect Saint?'
'Why isn't Father, the Superman, WE expected him to be?'
'Why are they only human?'
'Who am I?'
'Why am I here?'
Self.
Self.
Self.

Never a, 'How does Mum do it?'
'Day after day, month after month, year after year without end?'
Never once did we ask ourselves, 'How?' or even 'Why?'

Those hands, so aged now, crippled with arthritis,
Unable any longer, to even hold a pen,
And yet, as I work here,
In this far and distant land,
Those old hands send me their silent message,
By proxy.

'I can't write anymore, but otherwise I am well,
I hope and pray that you are too, my son,
I am your Mother,
I love you, may God bless.'

And with the warmth of their comforting message,
Those pained and crippled old hands,
Stroke a glow, into my exiled heart,
And squeeze a tear, from my lonely eye.

'I can't write anymore,
I am your Mother,
May God bless.'

God, that I could only say,
'Take my hands, Mother, they are strong,
Take this strong heart, I give it to you freely,
Use this younger healthier body, to ease your pain,
You own it, it's yours, I owe my life to you alone,
Take it all, you are so much more worthy of life than I,
Take it all, and live Mother, please, Live.'

Brother

For Lee

Brother, my brother,
So much part of each other,
The one who's so much like myself.

We are like candlesticks,
Smoky with age,
Separated, by the clock on the shelf.

I read what you write,
In the deadness of night,
You perceive all I'm trying to tell.

Perhaps it's not strange,
It's all been arranged,
That we draw from the very same 'well'.

Life seldom permits us,
The sharing of days,
We forfeit most things we have sought,

But life can't deny me,
My 'wish it had been'
It blooms fair, in my garden of 'thought'.

Separated by countries,
And oceans of years,
Destined to distance apart.

Yet, if I had my way,
We'd be 'young' and at 'play'
In the evergreen fields of my heart.

Aging

We are older, not yet old,
Not yet my brother,
Though we show the cursed signs of passing years,
Still with bodies strong,
And hearts set on the future,
We enter not that vale of ancient fears,

We have battled each his own,
This world of troubles,
And dined with tribulation for our fayre,
And where we've stepped, or slept or wept, or triumphed,
The echo of our names still lingers there.

We forced our ways through mountainous obstructions,
We walked the trail,
The lone trail oft we tread.
We have burned with pain,
And cursed this life and stumbled,
But there are lesser men, and lesser men are dead.

You have seen my naked pain,
And read my heartache,
And all your lifelong anguish shows in your eyes,
Where is the man would dare to call us failures,
Who's the fool would dare to criticise.

We have sons to pass our names through generations,
We can look on them with pride,
And watch them grow,
Though we often cast our seed on barren wasteland,
We can thank God for the fertile seeds we've sown.

Now our heads are grey,
Our faces stubbed and wrinkled,
Still the fires that forced us on are yet aglow,
It would take the whole world's oceans raised and scattered,
To attempt to douse these flames within our souls.

We have reached this year thus far, and shall go forward,
To whatever fate may hold, though good or bad,
And I want to say before we tread much further,
To have shared this life with you,
Has made me glad.

So, we shall dance at the weddings of our daughters,
We shall watch our sons stand tall and proud as men,
Although life yet may hold some troubled waters,
I'll be close to you, my brother and my friend.

Man on a Mountain

There is peace upon this mountain,
With the town so far below,
And sweet flows the water fountain,
As the soft caress of snow.

Here is my soul's tranquility,
And the tremor has ceased in my hands,
Down there, is nought but humility,
This life and its cursed demands.

I shall languish here on the mountaintop,
And drift with the soothing clouds,
I shall rest on this timeless mountain peak,
All dressed in these calm white shrouds.

The birds show quiet acceptance,
To my presence they bare no ill,
Yet my fellow man with a wave of his hand,
The last drop of blood would spill.

Oh to be as the tall pine tree,
Silent, and worldly wise,
To stand alone in need of none,
To betray or to criticise.

The birds would nest, in my evergreen boughs,
And the mountain would serve all my needs,
And never again would I need to walk,
As a man on the dangerous streets.

The Street

Born to the street, and grew,
Forced manhood, young and new,
A heart yet through and through,
Impassioned, clean and true.

Both 'Fate & Time' marched on,
The street, the street, was gone,
Turned my back with grief,
Sin choked behind locked teeth.

A heart, now through and through,
No longer clean and true,
A face became a mask,
Concealing all, its task.

No longer young, not young,
Torn hard 'twixt right and wrong,
What seemed so right, so right,
So strange with morning light.

This man, of forty years,
No slave to doubts or fears,
No longer cares, nor cares,
Both right and wrong forswears.

But, oft times there's the Street,
Soft memories repeat,
Quiet longings pierce me through,
For days, so simple, young, and true.

Orchestral Rains

I hear the music of the falling rain,
So like a symphony it sounds,
Tap tapping on my window-pane,
Slap slapping on the sodden grounds.

Crystal drops that tremble down the glass,
Their momentary art portray,
Pirouetting to the window-frame,
Dance to the ledge and simply fade away.

Percussion beats upon the sloping roof,
Fairy feet tap dancing in the spout,
The flames respond within the crackling fire,
Sparks that flash their moment then go out.

The Willow tree conducts the orchestra,
He dips and waves his leafy arms around,
Stretches and holds, the wind's crescendo builds
The oak and conifer, applaud the sounds.

The daffodils and roses nod and prance,
The rhododendron shakes his leaves with glee,
A multitude of blooms, in flowery dance,
To the magic rain that helps them blossom free.

And from the chimney pots, into the air,
A smoky ghost who manifests strange shapes,
He coils and spins, he twirls and swirls about,
I watch him ballet to the garden gates.

A whistle haunts me from within the house,
Another whirling spectre on the move,
The steamy spirit, from the kettle lid,
Glides to the ceiling and remains aloof.

The dripping maple sways hypnotically,
The rustling hedges whisper 'encore please'
But the big bass rainclouds start to drift away,
To let the gentle sun shine on the trees.

Such a way to spend a rainy day,
To let my fool's imagination run,
Call it childish but I've this to say,
When we were children, rainy days were fun.

Thoughts in the Firelight

Sitting in shadowed firelight,
No glaring electricity,
No TV thing blaring from the corner.

Only smouldering coals,
And occasional crackle of burning logs,
The clock,
Dutifully chimes the hour,
Then reluctantly lapses back into the incessant boredom,
Of wearing away our lives.
Tick, by countless tick.

You, there, in your favourite position,
Sat on the carpet, slippered feet in the hearth,
Resting your back on the armchair.

You sit quietly,
Gazing into the flame,
As though the glowing embers,
Contained therein,
The long withheld solution,
To all the woes and sorrows,
Of this your only life,
My wife of eighteen years.

I watch you,
In side profile,
Haloed, in flickering flame,
And see written on your soft features,
The age of our lives,
The reflection of my own years,
The pains and punishment,
Of a decade or more,
Spent mostly apart, in separate worlds.

You, here in our Belfast home,
And I, off tramping the globe,
Far, far, beyond your horizons.

It has never been easy, has it?
Never 'perfect'.

I know of all my numerous shortcomings,
Recognise my failings,
I realise fully,
That I,
Am somewhere opposite to 'wonderful'
On the measuring scales of life.

And you my love,
You are simply human,
A wife and a mother,
A victim of all the drudgery that entails,
Plus,
The inflicted loneliness,
Of my interminable absences.

Who are we,
You and I?
What are we doing,
And why do we do it?
Whatever 'it' may be.

There is a black hole.
At the centre of our personal little Universe,
Into it, we have poured,
Our lives,
Our love,
Our efforts.
And all their financial rewards.

Yet still,
It gnaws at us,
Greedy, insatiable, demanding,
Swallowing up our years,
Our pittance,
And sucking the very flesh from our bones.

But oh God,
Didn't we fight it though,
Don't we still!
It devours us, piece by bloody piece,
And we laugh in its slobbering face,
Let it go to hell,
We'll go out and have a beer, clink our proverbial glasses,
And live on smiling.

Look back and laugh,
Look forward and hope,
Educate our children with our deep scars of reminiscence,
Bear it all, and battle valiantly,
For the meagre morsels of joy,
We can choke out of this sad old world.

Yes, we have fought it,
Never winners,
But, survivors always.

No final victory to claim,
Life holds his trump card,
The evil joker, Time!
But shall we succumb?
Never!
Even with pain for sustenance,
Despair for dessert,
We shall fight the unending fight,
And smile that smile,
Through the smoky haze of uncertainty.

It hungers for us,
Lusts for control,
That monstrous, gulping, soul-swallowing void of hopelessness,
That deadly undertow.

We have fought it, tooth and nail,
Gaining ground, losing ground,
With the determination of undauntable souls.

We have raised our children,
Sheltered them through life's hurricanes,
Watched them grow, tall and strong,
We 'fed' them on our resistance,
Weaned them on, resilience, mercy, courage, compassion.

Taught them survival,
In the face of life's dangers,
And set them standing, feet planted firmly on earth,
On that treacherous, pot-holed road, to adulthood.

Eternally intertwined with the fabric of my heart,
Is my pride, my deep and honest love, for our children.

And now?
What will we do now,
That our children are almost grown?

We must remain the source of their strength,
Their axis, the hub of their wheel.

We shall watch over them,
Guide them still,
Bear them up should they fall,
Be there in the background raising their hopes should they
        weaken.

We must be their haven,
Their safety net,
As they climb the steep and hazardous face,
Of life's mountain.

Whilst you and I,
Journey ever downward,
On the declining slopes of age.

Yes,
I believe that's 'who' we are!
That's 'what' we are doing,
And 'they' our children,
Are 'why' we do it,
So then 'they' are what 'it' is all about!

My chain of thought,
Lingers in the glowing firelight,
My mind uncoils its sinewy tendrils,
Grasping at the fading images, of past and future,
But they scamper into shadowed corners,
Leaving me, in the clutch of the present.

I notice how your head slumps forward,
In the blessed heat of the fireside,
Weariness has taken you,
You sleep.

Rest my love, sleep on,
And dream of yesteryear,
When we were young,
And all the fire we needed,
Was ignited and blazing in our hearts!

When firelight danced in our eyes and in our hair,
Where now there remains the sparkle,
And approaching snows.

Sleep,
And dream of tomorrow,
When sweet grandchildren,
Will nestle on your breast.

Rest until the glow of our cosy firelight,
Is no more,
And shadows close in,
Like a threat.

Then waken!
To find me waiting here,
With the flames of hope,
Burning ever bright in my soul,
And my eyes, smouldering in the shadows,
Turned to the corridors of our future years.

(1988)

Silence

Your words were soft,
Whispered into the darkness.

'Don't go,' you said,
'When tomorrow comes, don't go.'

A simple request,
Sliping from the gentle lips,
I had just kissed.

'Don't go,' you said,
And with these words,
You send me to silence

I turn my face away,
There, in the darkness,
Cloaking my soul in shadow,
And look through the window.

Above the rustling trees,
A solitary star glistens,
In silver splendour.

The majesty of an unknown world,
Visible for a moment,
Before the night conceals it,
And all its mystery,
Behind a veil of dark and ominous cloud.

'Don't go little star,' I thought,
Why must all end with a leaving?
Why does dark cloud,
Screen the beautiful star?
Why does tonight only leave me tomorrow?
And why tomorrow,
Must I go where I wish not,
Leave when I should not?
Journey into aloneness,
When love and warmth lies here, beside me,
Beseeching me not to go,
Tomorrow, or ever,
And sending me to silence.

We lie quietly,
Together,
Touching in the afterglow,
Already apart,
And feeling the pain of all that is yet to happen.

'Don't go' so soft you whisper,
Once more,
And how should I respond to that?

To tell you all, that you already know?
That I must go,
That choice is a luxury for Kings and conquerors.

Your request pierces my feeble armour,
Stings my open wounds,
I feel the waning of all my spirit,
The treacherous desertion,
Of all my courage,

The draining of my resolve,
Heaving me mercilessly,
Into the pit of desolation.

If only . . .
I could . . .
Stay . . . Home!

'The children,' you say,

And I gasp into the night,
My chest tightens,
My eyes fill,
My heart plummets to even greater depths of despair.

'The children' you say,
Thus sending me to silence.

Outside, the rain begins,
As though the heedless sky should weep for my misery.

Somewhere, out on the lough,
A ship sounds her intentions,
Calling to the vast untamed oceans,
Her purpose,
Her leaving,
And heads out to sea.

The sky sends its loathsome message,
The evil drone of a lone aircraft,
Already high, in full flight,
Flying towards tomorrow, or forever.

Destiny awaits,
I am torn between her voice,
And your voice,
My life,
Pleading against my destiny.

'Don't go, the children'
'Please'.

Whispered words, soft, warm flesh,
The ship, the plane,
Dawn creeping in,
The clock ticking away this night and damning me to silence.

'Don't go,' you say, 'Please, it is morning'
'Come,' says the world, 'It is time.'

(*1986*)

Screams of Absence

Home again, to Ireland,
Basking in the warmth of wife and son,
God bless Ireland,
And dwell forever in our hearts and in our homes.

Driving down from the airport,
The car,
Screams an absence.

Onto Circular, my own domain,
Turn into the drive, and park.

My eyes are everywhere,
The garden, the boat, the house,
Home, home, home at last!

The house,
Screams an absence.

Anne, is here, my wife,
Jason is here, my son,
Where is April, my daughter?

April, little 'Bubbles'
Is in Donegal, with Angela,
Caravaning with the family Reid.

My heart,
Screams an absence.

These months were long,
From October through to March.

Spring approaches,
And 'Bubbles' is in Donegal.

The whole place broods,
And screams her absence.

Tomorrow, we go to Donegal.
To April.

Hard!
Hard months past,
Fraught with danger,
Cruel seas, heavy hazardous tasks,
In deep cold waters.

Mixed gas diving,
Damn all financial need,
Which dominates my life,
Dragging me to arid deserts and ocean depths.

While I burn and rage,
And ache, for my little family,
And all our people,
My sole ambition?
A life of my own.

I remember October,
Leaving my wife and kids,
Leaving my brother,
Complete with wife, daughter,
And two sons.

That awful November,
I rushed home,
A few days compassionate leave,
To a brother with wife, daughter,
One son,
And a small, undressed grave,
On a cold hill,
Marking the end,
Of a mere fifteen-year lifetime,
On this, harsh, unforgiving Earth.

No home coming for you,
Little Stuart,
A once only trip.

And we miss you,
I miss you,
My good days smile,
At your memory,
My bad days,
Scream your absence.

Never realized how much,
I took for granted,
Strong young boy,
Growing up fast,
Always be there,
No time now,
Always in a hurry,
Plenty of time 'later'
To relate to Stuart.

Now there is no 'later'
For you and I, Stuart.

And I want,
I really, really wish,
I want . . .
Well, Stuart,
I just want!

And I wish I could fly to you,
With return tickets for both of us,
You who gave up your life,
And I, who squander mine.

Ah child,
Do you know this pain you gave us?
Was it your wish to punish us so?
We are human too, Stuart,
And so very vulnerable.

It hurts, Stuart,
Oh God, but it hurts.

I took, a handful of soil,
From your small grave,
Put it in my pocket,
To seal in some container,
To keep and carry with me through all my travels.

Days later,
I reached into my pocket,
And brought forth, dry, powdery sand,

Which slipped through my fingers,
Like a symbolic accusation.

I held it in my palm,
And moistened it,
With my futile, useless and angry tears.

Left Ireland again,
All I ever do,
Mere days after standing by your graveside,
Left my family,
All of us grieving,
Struggling so,
With your loss.

Left you, little Stuart,
Forever,
Asleep on a cold hill.

And spent, a bitter lonely Christmas,
Again!
In the Middle East.

Now it's March!
I'm home, for a while,
And I'm off to Donegal,
To find 'Bubbles'.

Gathered little April in my arms,
And all the pain of these past months,
Recoiled into the background.

Hello, little daughter, how I love you,
All is well now, we are complete.

And Donegal is, soothing, mesmeric.

The Reids showed us around,
It's beautiful.

I stood, in those wild hills,
Purging dusty desert sands,
from Irish lungs. By breathing
deep the silver mists of Donegal.

A transfusion of Ireland,
Paddy's nectar, from Paradise,
Thank you Reids,
For this special introduction to Donegal.

It is a gift I shall cherish,
And remember you for,
A weekend in Dungloe,
With the family Reid!

I felt the mysticism, Dennis,
That cries aloud to your artist's soul.

Eating Anne Reid's salad,
And staring contentedly,
Out of your caravan window,
At the unspoilt Atlantic glory,
Of our own Ireland,
Thank you Reids.

When I leave again,
As inevitably,
I must,
And stand, once more,
On the burning desert floors of Arabia.

I shall think of all of you,
That weekend in Donegal.

And the thought of you there,
On those wild and lonely beaches,
Shall cool my burning flesh,
And bring shade,
To my exiled heart,
While it,
Screams of absence.

Father and Daughter

For April

Didn't I love you when you were wee,
Didn't I love you true,
Happily holding you there on my knee,
Loving each little gurgle and goo.

Didn't I love you, when you were small,
Didn't I love you still,
Though I sat up all night, chasing goblins from dreams,
Loved you then, as I always will.

Didn't I love you when you were six,
And you'd always run to me,
With little hurt fingers, or bumps on the head,
Or each little wounded knee.

Didn't I love you, at terrible ten,
When the 'dominance' started to show,
Didn't I love you, even more then,
Watching the 'womanence' grow.

Didn't I love you at tender fourteen,
Shocked by the hostile young girl,
Who suddenly struck with the edge of her tongue,
Devastating my heart and my world.

Didn't I love you at sweet sixteen,
And suddenly watching the boys,
Wasn't I sad, that it all had to end,
The 'little girl, Daddy, joys'.

Didn't I love you when I had to leave,
Begging God just to help me stay,
How could you know child, how sorely I grieved,
But life never showed me a way.

Now, don't I love the young woman you are,
Beautiful daughter, so fair,
Being a father, is a hard thing my child,
Loving you here, while you're far away, there.

Belfast, City of my People

In the town where I was born,
When first I heard the shipyard horn,
My wee heart from my breast was torn,
I thought the Banshees called.

The trams still ran on Belfast streets,
When first I tottered to my feet,
And World War Two was obsolete,
Sweet freedom now installed.

But life was really raw and tough,
What we possessed was small enough,
My folks worked hard and had it rough,
But that was Belfast's way.

My father was a shipyard man,
And he held neither dream nor plan,
Just sweat of brow and toil of hand,
Until his dying day.

My mother was a shipyard wife,
A harsh impoverished thankless life,
Her smiles were brief, her pain was rife,
We kids her only joy.

Oh how we wished to salvage them,
From hardship and a future grim,
'You work to eat, you sink or swim,
You'll learn that soon, my boy'.

And so I grew and went to school,
Ten years to learn the words of fools,
You must abide by all the rules,
Don't ever break the mould.

You don't do this, you can't do that,
You're just another shipyard brat,
In poverty you were begat,
Your story has been told.

Your tale is as your father's was,
And you'll do what he did because,
A son does what his father does,
And answers Harland's horn.

The son of a Belfast shipyard man,
A cog from a cog, in the master plan,
Your apprenticeship began,
The day that you were born.

You'll live your life devoid of hope,
You'll march the twelfth and kick the Pope,
And that's the full range of your scope,
'Tis how you'll live and die.

Be like many shipyard sons,
Who have no truck with priests or nuns,
And call no Catholic boys your chums,
Don't ask for reasons why.

But armed with questions in my youth,
I sought to find the vital proof,
That, 'Evil' was a Catholic truth,
And Chapel was their 'Coven'?

I heard the awful myths and tales,
At Catholic mass, a Prod's heart fails,
And they leap about with 'forks and tails'
Cooking Proddies, in an oven.

My boyhood friends were a hearty squad,
But often thought me rather odd,
'He can't tell Mickeys from a Prod,
Keep him quiet or he'll disgrace us.'

67

I walked the Shankill, walked the Falls,
And looking back my mind recalls,
The warmth and friendship 'twixt their walls,
In either of those places.

Now looking in the eyes of folk,
My mind perceives no joyous joke,
The bitter gall comes up to choke,
What has happened to our people?

Does God not smile on every church?
What faith in Him would God besmirch?
Or leave His faithful in the lurch,
'Neath cross or lofty steeple.

My people, it is time to look,
Once more into the oldest book,
And learn the awful path we took,
To turn on one another.

Jesus preached it, loud and clear,
His message travelled down the years,
'What you do to each man here,
You do to me, my brother.'

What good, possessing Ireland's soil,
What good, the hardship, pain and toil?
If hate and bloodshed should despoil,
The beauty of our nation.

What good, the claiming of this land,
By Protestant or Catholic hand?
If in the Eyes of God we stand,
Eternal in Damnation?

Death of Reason

Dreamed I climbed a stairway to the stars,
Watched the round blue orb of Earth, sedately spin,
Turned away and looked to open space,
That 'Nothingness' which beckoned me, 'come in'.

Threw a little pebble in the brook,
Watched the ripples skip and dance away,
Reached and felt the beating of my heart,
Thanked God I had lived to know this day.

Stood privileged in the presence of a flower,
Ached within, such beauty to behold,
Wandered through the snow, beside the lake,
Relished there, the mind reviving cold.

Standing sadly by an ancient fallen tree,
Wondered just what truth, that it might tell,
If trees and grass and birds could talk to man,
Would all within this world of ours be well?

Quite near, I heard the thunder of the guns,
Wings of death came screaming overhead,
Struck the towns where babes and mothers dwelled,
Heard the crying of the dying for the dead.

Silence came, with winds to clear the smoke,
Gentle snow fell, covering our shame,
Threw a little pebble in the brook,
Wondered, why some things, remain the same.

Divers in Saudi

Greed, aggression and tyranny,
Are the order of the day,
Evil lurks in the hearts of men,
Armies mass a short distance away.

Iraq has invaded her neighbour Kuwait,
And her forces dig in on the borders,
Once again the Allies unite,
And our troops are called to order.

Ahead lie the evils of carnage and death,
This may well be Iraq's darkest hour,
We ex-patriot hordes, hold our visions of home,
Midst the winds that whisper war.

The free world unites to withstand the threat,
And the rhetoric echoes the Earth,
While the merciless sun burns us through to the bone,
And we long for the lands of our birth.

But the oil must flow, so down we go,
To the depths, despite danger or fear,
For this is the Gulf, and we've known long enough,
That death is most constantly near.

So we dive and we work, not a man tries to shirk,
The world needs its oil every hour,
In these deep seas, alone, divers dream of their home,
While the winds, they whisper war.

(August 1990)

Simple Prayer

You gave us this world Lord, with all of its ails,
And all of its mysteries to solve,
We're not doing so well Lord, destruction's at hand,
Are You going to stand by, uninvolved?

Don't let all these people die Lord, please,
Lord can You hear me pray?
All of the wrongs Lord, that mankind has done,
You can undo, in a day.

Millions of soldiers, with terrible weapons,
Are facing their foes on these borders,
And hundreds of thousands, even millions may die,
Unless You've countermanded their orders.

Now I know we're all sinners, we don't deserve much,
And shame keeps my eyes, on my feet,
And I wonder my Lord, do You ever know shame?
When the small children die in the streets.

We've had two world wars Lord, and nobody gained,
But millions of people were lost,
And the weapons back then wouldn't rate with today's,
Who'll be left Lord, to tally the cost?

What's it all for Lord, another world war,
Is that how man's destined to end?
I have always believed, You were King of all kings,
And that man had the Friend of all friends.

You say 'Faith' can move mountains, it can also be shook,
And I fear if You stand idly by,
And let man tear down the Creation You've built,
Men may think Your existence, a lie.

71

So I pray to You Lord, don't let more people die,
Lord can You hear me pray?
If You do Lord, You might as well fold up the world,
Just fold it, and throw it away.

Look into the eyes of an innocent child,
Look at the babes in their cots,
Though He died here on Earth Lord, You still have Your Son,
Would you take all the wee ones we've got?

Stop all the wars Lord, make them take all their guns,
Melt them down into ploughshares again,
Send health to the ailing, and food to the poor,
And to lands facing drought, send the rain.

There is so much to learn Lord, that we don't understand,
We are stumbling oh God be our Crutch,
Open our eyes, make us children again,
Cleanse us oh Lord with Your Touch.

'Suffer the children . . .' Your very own words,
'. . . the children to come unto Me.'
Since You love them so much Lord, then don't let them die,
Let them live, let the children be free.

ACH. I don't have the words Lord, I'm the wrong kind of man,
But Lord, if You hear me pray,
Send us the good Herald Angels of Peace,
Before some madman turns us to clay.

(January 13th Saudi Arabia)

The Diver

Shall it end . . . ever?
Oh God, that I might surface,
Be done with these waters,
This Gulf,
These, interminable wars.

And go home.

I am a dweller of the seas,
Farflung, from the threshold of my life.

A distant, unclaimed,
Solitary, silent swimmer of the Deep.

The Old Diver

I've been down in the deep,
My bonnie lads,
I've been under the sea with the fishes,
And I've found me a corpse which was rotting bad,
Seen how 'Davy Jones' deals with such dishes.

I have dived into caves,
Hidden under the waves,
I've seen sights such as words won't describe them,
Where men dived for pleasure,
And some dived for treasure,
But then, leaving those caves was denied them.

I have seen strange things,
My bonnie lads,
Poison sea snakes, the shark and the 'cuda,
And I've known all the fears,
That a man ever feels,
For I've dived off the coast of Bermuda.

I've been down in the deep,
My bonnie lads,
I've been under the waves with the fishes,
And I've found me a corpse which was rotting bad,
Seen how 'Davy Jones' deals with such dishes.

I have dived on the wrecks,
Those which never came back,
I've found ships without crews, yet still sailing,
And I've dived in the deep,
Where their souls will not sleep,
Where I've heard their blood-curdling wailing.

I'll be diving tomorrow,
As usual, my lads,
To the deck now for fresh air I'm walking,

And not one more word,
Will you squeeze from me lads,
For I've scared myself shitless, just talking.

Voice of the Masses

Explain for us, if you will,
The philosophy behind present day,
nuclear capacity for destruction.

Has the rapid development of man's,
Supertechnological ability,
simply taken us that crucial giant leap forward,
to extinction?

May we, the people speak?
May we, refuse participation,
In whose trembling hand
Lies the continuance or cessation
of our existence,
Why this creation of tools for mass genocide?

Must we cooperate,
Simply bow our heads and wait,
to die passively, without say,
without consideration,
without voice, choice, or protest?

Shall our bones murmur on the winds of the nuclear night
that this mutilation,
this annihilation,
this desecrating death of deaths,
was, is, preferable to the life we live?

And when the yet unborn
come to us,
with final deliverance,
the 'Sacred promise'
Shall they weep over our past world,
beat their breasts and cry out to us,
'Too late, too late'.

But shall we only in silence lie,
rotting and still,
consumed by the corruptions of our trusted leaders in power,
banished to oblivion by man's psychopathic technology gone
    amok,
HEAR US.
for we SHALL speak.

Give unto God, that which is God's.

But unto Caesar, render no power
over life death, or the Atom.

From Dunglow to the Desert

I wrote 'Donegal' with my fingertip,
In the desert sand on the gunnel,
And I wrote it again on the stack of the ship,
In the soot that falls from the funnel.

Once again there is desert war,
And home is beyond my call,
But I close my eyes from reality,
And see the shores of Donegal.

Where the small Sandpiper sings,
And the white Gulls on the wing,
The Atlantic waves roll shoreward, long and slow,
There's the scent of burning turf,
And the sound of pounding surf,
If I could fly, I'd wing my way to sweet Dunglow.

Beneath this fierce Arabian sun,
The massing has begun,
Of troops and arms, an awesome war machine,

And across the blue, so clear,
Fly the warplanes, low and near,
And I wish to God this land I'd never seen.

But where the small Sandpiper sings,
And the white Gulls on the wing,
Where Atlantic waves roll shoreward, long and slow,
There's the scent of burning turf,
And the sound of pounding surf,
How I wish I could return to sweet Dunglow.

The Great Deterrent

When all the world is laid to waste,
And civilization's gone,
When all we have is devastation to reflect upon.

When humanity's survivors say,
'We must begin again',
I wonder will they stop and think,
Why we did those things back then.

To build such hideous weapons,
Their only purpose to destroy,
Then, to place them in the hands of maniacs,
Who jump for joy.

'We'll buy all your wondrous weaponry,
Though you know we'll never pay,
But we'll turn your own germ warfare,
And your nukes on you someday.'

Did we think it didn't matter,
That those bombs were built to use?
And though we were their creators,
Could be first to be abused.

Now it seems it's going to happen,
The maddened beast is at our doors,
And the tools of trade he uses,
Once were mine and once were yours.

Well, we talked about deterrents,
Then went arming all mankind,
Now Saddam Hussein has awesome power,
And it's blown his twisted mind.

The Five Sentence Existence of Man

God created man, from dust of the Earth,
Man split the Atom,
Man created Nuclear warfare,
Man's Nuclear warfare, created ashes,
Ashes to ashes, dust to dust.

As I am Judged

Upon your lofty pedestal, you sit,
And glowering down, unpack your judgement kit,
Judging me, the lowly damned, who takes a drink,
Yet would I balk and fear,
Your hypocritic thoughts to think.

You see me through your dark veiled judging eyes,
I represent the very wrong whom you despise,
And so you don the 'grieving cloth' upon your head,
And quote what will become of me when dead.

My mind and soul shall rise above your condemnation,
For I accept me, as I am, my lowly station,
I won't believe some skulking God,
Hides cloaked in cloud,
Whom you claim to represent, and preach out loud.

The, God, I know comes not to sunder, but to save,
And should I cart my drinker's breath,
Into my grave,
I shall not die, believing 'Hell's' my destined place,
Lest he condemn me eye to eye,
And face to face.

Harsh Judgement

'He was always too fond of the bottle' they'd say,
'By far much to keen on the brew',
'But so was his father before him' they'd say,
'Drink to that family's not new'.

'Eventually the liquor will kill him' they'd say,
'The Whiskey will drown him for sure',
'He'll never be blessed, till he gives it a rest',
'No, he'll die Whiskey sodden and poor'.

He'd hear them each day, as he walked on the street,
On his way down the road to the bar,
Or behind curtained windows, in the dark of his home,
Where he hid from their world for an hour.

He knew in their eyes he was lower than low,
He accepted their lowly esteem,
He knew he would never stand tall in their eyes,
These people, they lived in a dream.

The Cancer, was eating him down to the bone,
The pain nearly drowning him sure,
Wave after wave of pure pain without rest,
So much more than a man could endure.

He craved the oblivion, alcohol brought,
Harming no one, he drank pain away,
He'd drift through his nights in a dull drunken haze,
Till the pain would return with the day.

He wished in his heart, that the Whiskey would kill,
Wished he could die from the drink,
It would prove them all right, for the things that they say,
And justify, all, that they think.

The Drinker

Alone at the bar, in this silent hour,
I gaze at the brew in my glass,
The barman smiles, and makes to converse.
But wise, lets the strange moment pass.

I sip for a while, remembering a child,
Who detested the mere smell of drink,
An ironic smile, for I was that child,
Now into the bottle I sink.

What brings me to this, what is it I miss?
For I loathe the pathos of a drunk,
Yet it draws me right back, like there's something I lack,
And down into the whirlpool I've sunk.

Riddled with guilt, the froth of youth spilt,
Waste now beyond my control,
Do I seek here at last, consolation in glass?
As the brew to my wet lips I tilt.

If I'm worried, I drink!
If I'm happy, I drink!
I drink when I'm feeling good.

I drink to forget,
I drink with regret,
I drink, 'cos I'm just in the mood.

It's a social event, what do people resent?
Where is the offence I commit?
Won't they ever relent, with their hints and comments?
Won't they leave me in peace for a bit.

Why am I cursed with insatiable thirst?
Why do I feel so confused?
Why do I shake with each breath I take?
But the alienation's the worst.

Now I'm loathe to confess, but it's all such a mess,
'Hey barman, another glass here'
Sure I'll just have a drink, then I'll be in the pink,
There are plenty of grapes in the press.

The more drink I have, then the louder I'll laugh,
And an evening slips by very fast,
So open a bottle and break out a keg,
God knows, sure it might be my last.
Aye, God knows, sure it might be my last.

Paranoid Alcoholism

Catch me if I fall,
My world's unstable,
The very earth, trembles beneath my feet.
But only the patch on which I stand, it seems,
As people around are heedless,
To the vibrant tremors,
Running all through my body.

Someone, look my way,
And, please,
Catch me if I fall.

Hold unto me,
Feel it pulling?
The vortex?
Edging me towards,
The gaping,
Madly spinning,
Deep black hole.

No one sees,
But that evil void,
That yawning hungry chasm,
Is sucking at my being,
Drawing me,
Enticing me,
To enter space unknown.

Don't let go,
Hold me tight,
Oh God,
I'm sinking.

Why are my days,
A parody of life?
Why these choking fears,
That snarl and bite,
Like some rabid, raging animal?

Why?
Do I sweat, in the cold?
Shiver, in the heat?
Why, when I lie down to my rest,
Does my head spin so?
And why, when I stand,
Does all else stagger,
And lean,
Sickeningly,
Unbalanced?

Why, do I crave,
A fullness of stomach?
Then,
Vomit, when I eat?
Now, all is quiet,
Quiet as the grave,
Yes,
Peace, for a while,
Peace?

But, listen . . . listen,
How ominous, this soundlessness,
Quiet . . . so quiet,
Why?
Oh stop this petrifying stagnancy,
Don't you feel it?
The very air is filled with menace,
Oh but I fear it so,
This cloistered, clutching, claustrophobic quiet,
Oh God,
Deliver me from this tortuous stillness,
I am suffocating in this, torpid silence.

I need,
Air!
People!
Sound!
Movement!
Shout, oh please,
Have the people shout,
Sing and dance,
Don't leave me all alone,
In this world of nothingness,
No please, the creatures will come,
To torment me, don't leave me.

Ah, voices,
Doors banging, and voices,
Laughter,
Glorious noise,
Hear the people laugh, Ha Ha, yes,
Better, much, much better,
Isn't it,
Isn't it?
Isn't it better?

But, listen . . . listen,
Why do they laugh so?
Laughing, laughing, loud laughter,
Coming closer, closer,
Coming toward me,
What do they want?
They are laughing at me, aren't they?
Yes, some evil scheme is afoot,
Listen, oh listen,
Those voices,
The cackle of swarms from Hell!

I cannot bear it,
The sound.
Evil, evil laughter,
Oh stop it please,
Someone stop them,
Don't let them get to me,
With deadly laughter,
Somone save me,
Someone.

Hold me please,
Catch me if I fall.

Help me, you will help me, won't you?
Listen . . . listen,
There is danger, . . . everywhere,
Trust, no one!
I, trust no one!
People, frighten me,
They frighten me!

Why . . . why do you stand so near?
Holding me . . . gripping me,
You are keeping me here,
Against my will,
You are . . . one of . . . Them!
You mean me harm,
I see it now,
Let go of me,
Stand back,
Leave me alone.
Why do you touch me?
You might be diseased,
Evil, who are you?
I am hot, so hot,
Get away from me.

I am falling, tumbling, falling,
Catch me!
Don't go please,
The quiet,
The vortex,
The darkness,
I am sinking,
Help me Oh God!
Catch me, catch me,
Catch me when I fall.

The Migrant Mind

Austere are my surroundings, on this vessel,
A little cabin, empty as a cell,
As naked as this wide unbroken ocean,
As Spartan as someplace a Monk might dwell . . . as is,

My mind, adrift, somewhere out in eternity,
I have shackled it, and tried to chain it still,
Futile are all bonds I've placed upon it,
For it wanders through the Universe at will.

Upon this Earth remains this useless body,
Struggling fruitlessly, to blunder on alone,
And the world tries hard in vain to keep in contact,
But my mind is seldom 'home' to 'lift the phone'.

The everyday inanities of living,
The boredom and the bullshit, get me down,
I stand like some vacated automaton,
While my mind upon some mystic plain, abounds,

In this world I am a lost and hopeless misfit,
And it hurts those ones, I've never wished to hurt,
I am left with an abandoned floundering body,
Which my mind is sore determined to desert.

There is mystery and intrigue 'neath these Heavens,
There are answers, treasured knowledge to be found,
And the greatest secrets yet revealed to mankind,
Weren't discovered, with our noses to the ground.

I am scarcely ever with you now, my people,
A wilderness of bone and flesh that toils,
I breathe, I walk, I talk and work among you,
I care nought, for the dividing of the spoils.

90

So those moments then, when you shall find me missing,
I have not fled from you, forevermore,
My mind is somewhere off, on quest for answers,
In search of all my soul has hungered for.

Forgive me, if I'm distant, dim, and vacant,
Understand, at times I'm just not there,
Be assured, this 'state' is not one of my choosing,
My fleeting mind has roamed at will since birth.

And so . . .

Austere are these chambers of my spirit,
Little rooms wherein I seldom dwell,
As vacant as the gulf betwixt the planets,
This heart, this flesh, are empty as a shell.

Little Leaf

The last golden leaf,
Shivers far out on a limb,
There are no more,
All have succumbed to approaching Winter winds.

The little leaf is beaten,
Twisted and whipped,
Snapped and broken,
Thrown to the ground.

I too shall be severed from the place of my birth,
And thrown to the winds.

While you, little leaf,
Lie crushed and dying,
Blown by the wayside,

I shall be tossed on the seas,
Bitten by the winds,
Lashed by the waves,
And lonely for home.

We both die a little,
Every year,
Crumpled and aging,
With time and its remorseless winters.

But, no matter little leaf,
God willing,
We shall return,
Together,
In the spring.

Paddy's Destiny

I had mountains to climb, so I climbed them,
Oceans to cross, so I sailed,
I had victories to claim, so I claimed them,
Failures to face, so I failed.

I had women to love, so I loved them,
Children to sire, so I did,
I had heartache to bear, so I bore it,
So much joy, which I found in my kids,

I had years hurry by, how they hurried,
Too few at home, lots away,
Life hustles me on in a fury,
How I wish I could stop for a day.

There are moments of Grace I remember,
Other moments which pierce me with shame,
Love that glows in my soul, like an ember,
When I haven't a friend to my name.

Indescrible lone- ness, I've lived it,
In lands far and strange, which I've roamed,
I've been emigrant, transient and exile,
Wanting nothing on Earth, but my home.

'Paddy's destiny' permit me to call it,
When I fly, with cold stone in my heart,
There is no one on whom I would blame it,
Life just held it in store from the start.

How I wish this old world, could be different,
Wish I could change, but I can't,
How I wish I could reach out to people,
Wish I could learn what they want.

How I wish I could say, what I'm feeling,
Wish all my troubles would end,
This old life keeps you turning and reeling,
Wish my loved ones, could still be, my friends.

How I wish this old heart could be printed,
So that page after page they could read,
And at last understand, its true content,
And help heal these wounds, that so bleed.

Hope

Hope is all I have,
To see me through my darkest night,
Hope helps me live,
Through my most dreaded days,
Hope is there, when the hardships seem intolerable,
And comforts me, in the valleys of death.

Hope,
Has been my life's faithful companion,
It never leaves me,
Through cold years, walked alone,
It has raised me,
When the world crushed my spirit,
Hope brought to me,
My day of freedom,
When my courage stood on the precipice,
My battered body,
On the threshold of submission.

Hope has kept my back straight,
My heart strong,
My determination secure,
When I was laden with troubles,
Burdened with care,
And wounded to my soul.

I shall sleep this night,
With hope in my heart,
Shall rise tomorrow,
With hope for the new day,
I shall toil through my weariness,
Through all my tomorrows,
With bright burning hope,
For the years ahead,

And Christ shall sustain me,
For He is my only hope,
My eternal hope,
All the hope I'll ever need.

Lord, To Be A Child Again

That child who will not die,
Still comes to me,
And locks into my peace of mind,
Accusingly.

Saying.
I am who you were,
So what became of me?
I see naught of myself in you,
But, chains I see.

For all I ever loved,
Believed and hoped in faith,
Was buried while alive,
Beneath the you of late.

You are the imposter who took away my life,
And locked me,
In your sin-filled tomb,
As dark as night.

Although I'm sore restrained,
You keep me buried here,
Deep within your heart,
You know I'm ever near.

I am all that represents,
The good in you,
And I'm the one who suffers most,
For all you do.

The dark side of your soul,
That part you will not see,
Is hidden well by Mercy's veil,
Of secrecy.

But someday, someway,
You'll be forced to face yourself,
To realize you're balanced,
On a sloping shelf.

With all reserves depleted,
You will reach that place,
And see at last your destiny,
In time and space.

And when at last you weary,
Having failed the test,
You will seek a place of solace,
Where your soul may rest.

And I, who never wronged you,
Though you buried me,
Shall castigate you sore,
Before I set you free.

For I'm the child, beneath the face,
Of every man,
And most men have to die,
Before they understand.

That if you'd let my innocence,
Survive with you,
You would not have to face this fate,
Life's brought to you.

Innocence conceives no ill,
No evil does,
If you could only change what is,
For all that was.

Perhaps you'd be so wise,
To get it right this time,
And hesitate to take away,
What once was mine.

For I am all that represents,
The good in you,
I am 'innocence' the sacrifice,
You'll learn to rue.

The Giant Oak

Never, a mere tree,

A strong, proud and powerful King,
Holding aloft,
In his mighty arms,
The myriad subjects,
Of his leafy Kingdom.

Car Wreck

Evil, dust covered old relic,
Stationary at last,
Bleeding rust,
Puking oil,
And voiding a brown slime of radiator water,
Peeling paintwork,
Too dull to reflect the sunlight,
Stripped of all splendour,
Chrome cracked,
Headlamps gone, seats slashed,
Tyres deflated in final humility,
Registration 666,
The number,
Of,
The immobilised beast.

Old Rope

Coil of old rope,
Tangled and twisted,
Into a quagmire,
Of hopeless confusion,
Like,
The City Underground.

Low Spirits

Oh melancholy, morose, sad circumspection,
Depart hence, from this thoughtful room,
You dull my mind, you cause me frown,
You have me age too soon,
I have not lived a morning yet,
Wouldst thou have me die by noon?

Contradiction

Churchbells are ringing for Christmas,
Happy hearts, singing in the New Year.

While somewhere a bell tolls in mourning,
And little children's hearts, tremble in fear.

Prayer Of The Working Man

I have carried the load of the working man,
Gave my all for the working man's shillin',
But there's little to show for the sweat and toil,
While around me the rogues make a killin'.

What can you buy with a principle?
How do you cook self-respect
What can you leave for your children someday?
'Cept this burden you hump on your back.

Where's the reward for the years of hard work?
How much must you earn to buy leisure?
But hardship's the cup, we continually sup,
And you swallow it measure by measure.

So much for the 'heritage' built for the kids,
By determined and dogged endeavour,
Before a pound's gained, this world has it claimed,
And your pocket's left light as a feather.

Now I've never sought wealth, I've a preference for health,
But I seek for the substance to live,
No financial stress, and the right to take rest,
And a little left over to give.
Each man has his ways and I've spent all my days,
In pursuit of that moment of pleasure,
When my family well fed, owns the roof overhead,
And it's theirs for their comfort, to treasure.

Now I've seldom complained, while my young years remained,
But I'm forty and progress is slow,
I'll sing honesty's praise, if the question is raised,
But I'd like to have something to show.

This old world has its hand, in the midst of my plan,
And seems ever determined to thwart me,
Though I'm worked to the bone and weary for home,
There is seldom a rest to reward me.

I'm as lean as a post, yet work harder than most,
While the rogues gather wealth and grow fat,
I won't injure, or steal, keep my nose to the wheel,
Tell me Lord how to justify that.

So what say You, Lord? I took You at Your word,
But we don't present much of a case,
If honesty's best, how come all the rest,
Seem to coin it and laugh in my face?

Now I've prayed here all night, I suppose it's not right,
For a man to ask God for a favour,
So forgive me, my God for behaving so odd,
I must rise now and go to my labour.

Perhaps we're not meant, to have more than the 'rent',
Or the price of a loaf on the table,
So accept my thanks please, for the blessing of these,
And the strength, that to earn them I'm able.

1969 . . .

was the last dance of youth,
on a narrow street called 'Young'
and before I could regain my breath,
my youth had come and gone,

for youth is such a fleeting thing,
never ours to keep,
and 'young' is an enchanted dream
which slips away in sleep,

my heart still sings
my soul has wings
my hair is thin and grey,
yet my memory still wanders,
through those years of yesterday.

My eyes lock on the future,
and my steps are forward all,
my persistent mind takes flight at will
to golden days I still recall.

A fool can lose reality,
let the present slip away,
by looking back too longingly,
to a long gone summer's day.

Yet somehow, in the darkest night,
alone inside your head
your movie reel of memories,
insists on being played.

And there he is, remembered youth,
walking heedless through your years,
his mind so full of hopes and dreams,
his heart devoid of fears.

The one who chose the steps you took
whose sad mistakes you made,
who danced you to that narrow street,
where youth began to fade.

To that last sweet year of '69
when 'Young' street passed with time,
and 21 'Married Ave' would hold you to your prime.

This old world turned
and changed that too, and still the years march on,
now once again you take the steps,
alone towards the dawn.

Whatever fate the future holds,
what'er might come and go
the 'yesteryouth' shall stalk your thoughts
to and fro, and to and fro.

Down that little narrow street,
up 'Married Ave'
along the open highway,
when once again, there's only you.

He's to blame for each mistake
for all that might have been
for every wasted hope you had
and every broken dream.

For every hurt you ever caused
for every day you squandered
for every love you tossed away
each heart you tore asunder.

He committed every sin,
and every deed that shamed you
and angered every one you knew
who criticised or blamed you.

Lay all your guilt there,
at his feet,
and pass on him your sentence
and see if you can draw from him
a whisper of repentance.

And when he bows his head in pain
convicted cursed and damned,
face the truth about yourself
that 'he' was 'who' I 'am'.

Looking back holds joy and pain
as so with each tomorrow
for every tear there'll be a smile
for every love, a sorrow

for every day of dark despair
there'll be a day of pleasure
your 'yesteryouth' and you have learned,
that 'time' is your greatest treasure.

Tir Na Nog

There is a land somewhere,
Beyond the vale of my fears,
Through the forests of my confusion,
Across the oceans of my dreams,
And on, and on,

Oh to travel there someday,
Burden free in solitude,
Light of heart and hopeful,
Sea wind in my face,
Salt air on my lips.

On fast currents of blue waters,
Over white topped waves and golden shores.

High above mountain peaks,
Snow capped and gleaming,
Green lands and tumbling rivers,
Westward, always west.

Westward beyond the Emerald,
On winds that whisper freedom,
Freedom of the heart, the mind, the soul.

Past seabirds singing,
Of the distant Isle,
Across the cold Atlantic,
And on, and on,

To an island in the silver mist,
Magical,
Mythical,
Mysterious.

Far from the pulsing press,
Of impoverished peoples,
Far from the mounting madness of the masses.

My one wish,
My dream desire,
Long lost sanctity,
In the legendary Land of the Young,
The land of Tir Na Nog.

The Launching

And in the silken silent solar system,
Stars glisten like angels' tears,

The moon shines sadly,
Serenely,
Somnambulantly on,

As brave, solitary little Ulysses,
Flies fearlessly forward,

Searching seeking, probing,
Towards the forbidden, fiery curtained,
Flame veiled secrets,

Of the Sun.

(October 1990)

The Hunchback

Look at him there, bent and fumbling,
And shuffling around, in his shack,
Imagine his thoughts, as he's stumbling,
Neath that burden, he bears on his back.

Why is there love, and love to spare,
In the heart of an ugly man?
Why the flame in his groin, why the stir in his loins,
Needs, there's no one to understand.

How can a man have the heart of a Prince,
And the passions of Byron's, 'Don Juan'?
When he's shunned by the females of all size and shapes,
Cos life made him an ugly man.

Why is he blessed with intellectual prowess?
He's as gentle and warm as a lamb,
He's so full of desire, his poor heart is on fire,
Not a woman alive gives a damn.

He's a man who resides neath two mountains,
One which reaches the clouds, cloaked in trees,
And the other which presses its weight on his back,
Till it bends both his spine and his knees.

Why is this life such a puzzle, I ask,
And why must he suffer so?
This twisted warped thing, has the mind of a King,
Grotesque looks, hide the good of his soul.

Yet he moans not his suffering, nor curses at God.
He calls it 'the hand' he was dealt,
Forced to stare at the ground, as he hobbles around,
And I think of the rage I'd have felt.

He is destined to loneliness, and the celibate's life,
He will never know touch of a girl,
He will never sire children, or sleep close to a wife,
Didn't Christ,
Pay the sins of this world?

A Vapor Trail

A vapor trail,
Product of some invisible hand.

A slash of white,
Across the blue expanse,
Of cloudless sky.

Lingering,

Lingering,

Scattered to infinity,
By the breath of the Universe, and gone forever.

The spoken word,
A mere gasp of air,
Spat from the lips, unheeded, unheard, soon forgotten,
And gone forever.

Of such,
Finite things,
Are we lowly mortals made.

A spoken word,
A lingering moment,
A dispersing vapor trail,

Lost, on the wind, and gone forever.

The Escapist

Beyond the veil of human vision,
A better world there's got to be,

Someplace the human eye can't see,
Yet but a blink from you and me,

A close of the mind so the Pineal eye,
Can transport the soul beyond the sky,

To somewhere Earthly time can't spy,
Inflicting age and a day to die,

Some gentle warm Elysian Isle,
No pain, no fear, no tears to cry,

A place where children blossom and smile,
And the hearts of men are as pure as a child's,

Where women can live in equality,
And every race is strong and free,

No class, no war, no hypocrisy,
No power in the hands of insanity,

I dream of such a Utopia,
Human kind in euphoria,

A blessed peaceful Shang-gri-La,
A Tir Na Nog, God's Heaven.

Tainted Angel

'Anything you want to do to me for £20.'

I turned toward the small voice,
And looked at her there, all five feet of her,
On a cold and windswept winter street.

A tainted angel, alone in a city of drizzle and damp,
Scantily clad and shivering,
Trembling with apprehension, cold and hunger,
Someone's daughter, fifteen to sixteen years old,
As young as my own.

'Anything you want mister, but don't hurt me please.'

'Where is your home?' I asked, 'Your parents?'

'You a cop?' Question for a question.

'You are a cop.' Worried statement.

'No, not a cop, a parent, now why don't you go home.'

'If it's the money mister, I'll do it for £15.' she said.

What a world, fifteen year old experienced whore,
cutting the cost of her own degradation,
haggling for defilement.

'£15 just don't hurt me mister.'

Hurt you, I couldn't hurt you, anymore than I can help you.

And who would I be to judge you little girl,
If by some miracle I could change your world
send you clean and fresh, happily unsullied
into the home of some decent, stable and caring
parents, who would nurture you, cherish you and
guide you.
If only I could wish you to some saving Grace
you poor soiled and shaking product of lost Paradise,
despairing of hope and home.
A premature fallen angel.

So, God, . . . tell me what to do for this child,
You know, 'Suffer the little children' etc, etc,

Well then, tell me what to do.
You are the God of mercy, and love,
Well? . . .
It does seem sometimes, as though you are a God
of determined silence.

Should I take her home?
Present her to my wife, saying, 'Look, I've brought home
this adolescent slut to share our lives, because I fancy
myself as a great redeemer'
And she shall live in our marriage with our fine tall son
our clean and lovely young daughter, and we shall teach
her a better life.'

And would my wife be impressed by my kindness,
would she rejoice?
I think not.
Rather she would decide I had finally taken
leave of my limited senses.

And the child? Would we save the child?
Or would she destroy us?

'Do you want me or not mister? £15 where's your car?
I'll give you a good time I'm experienced.'

Visions of squalid back seats, steamy windows
to hide her sad debasement.

'Here is ten pounds, go buy a hot meal, and get off
the streets before you get hurt or arrested.'

And so that I don't feel a father's responsibility,
so I can walk away without guilt,
£10 to appease my conscience,
who is the cheaper, she or I?

'I'll earn the money mister, don't want charity.'

'Aren't you just a little too cold and hungry,
too wet and miserable for demonstrations of
false pride? Take it and go.'

Yes, so who would I be to judge you child,
selling your young body to survive,
You make the world a lonelier place,
inflicting me with guilt and anguish,
I would be no party to the destruction
of your youth and beauty, and past innocence.
But I am male, and guilty by association.

Small creature of the night, tragic and trembling,
I am saddened for you on your cruel street corner.

Though perhaps if you knew me, you might be a little
sad for me, my fallen angel.
We are alike in obscure ways,
You, who sells her body to survive,
And I who sell my life,

You a lost and wayward premature tainted angel,
And I,
A soul in chains.

Grim Harvest

Kings and clowns and conquerors,
Knights in shining armour,
Fair young maids in leafy glades,
The plough boy and the farmer.

Duke or Count or common man,
Or Lord of these lands over,
Happy lass, or priest at mass,
Or wild eyed gypsy rover.

The Reverend, the Highwaymen,
Bold pirates on the seas,
Zulu queen, or sweet colleen,
Or Nun on penitent knees.

Evangelist, or damned or blessed,
The meek or Herculean,
The master or the miser,
Or the prisoner bound and beaten.

Sailor Jack who changed his tack,
To love a sweet Tahitian.
Or Tom and Dick who labour quick,
Or Harry 'Incompletion'.

Vagrant tramp or teenage scamp,
Or mistress in her tower,
Men of fury, Judge or jury,
Or old maid bent and sour.

The robber or the radical,
The rebel on the run,
The Clergy at Sabbatical,
The man behind the gun.

Killer, miller, chimney sweep,
Tinker tailor spy,
The old man from the mountain,
Who is coming down to die.

Whiteman, blackman, Jain or Jew,
Or yellow Oriental,
Or Eskimo from lands of snow,
Or Latin Continental.

Men of God or evil men,
Or Ladies of the night,
There was not one, since time begun,
Could set this world to right.

All skin and flesh and blood and bone,
Has but a common end,
We live we love, we ache we die,
We're all the same, good friend.

Cause no grief, inflict no pain,
Promote not persecution,
Nor bring to misery any man,
Nor child to destitution.

No woman strike, no child abuse,
No slavery, pay your servants,
For all your deeds are planted seeds,
And Christ is all observant.

Believe that life's a sacred thing,
Good Shepherd be our Keeper,
Lest we should damn our souls to be,
Grim Harvest for the Reaper.

Silence of the Stars

Shall I dine out in the Universe,
With the foolish Virgin Seven,
To light their lamps,
Ignite their fires,
And fill their wombs with leaven.

Shall Saturn's sisters quench this thirst,
These silken sirens of the stars,
Or Neptune's tempting nieces,
With their soft seductive powers.

Drink,
To Uranus,
His nebulous, young harem,
Hazily hidden,
To transcend into that sanctum,
Taste the bliss of his forbidden.

Let me find aloft, a love,
Christ cleansed of all unholy,
Sanctify this soul,
With age and sin receding slowly.

Let me shed my human guise,
And cast it far, far from me,
Corrupted flesh, and sorry heart,
And all that's overcome me.

Grant me flesh that's spirit pure,
Extract me from the mire,
With purple sequined irises,
And lips like furnace fire,
And clean untainted, puritanical, sexspiritual desire.

Place me in that Hand which wrought the red canals of Mars,
And fire me like an arrow,
Through the forests of the stars.

Let me glimpse the Child,
Who rides the silver swans of Heaven,
Render me of purist spirit,
Transfigured and forgiven.

Set my course amidst the stars,
Which light the galaxies, between us,
To taste the scarlet grapes of Jupiter,
The bluest wines of Venus.

Set me free to seek one year,
From June to flowering June,
The flaming Phoenix of the Sun,
White Eagles of the moon.

On the Golden whale that swims the seas,
Of some unmanned Paradise,
Let me glide the Silver Seed,
To where new Eden lies.

Fly me to some alien Orb, where blossoms Springs eternal
        flowers,
And let me dance my death amidst the silence of the stars,
With harmony, and rhapsody, a symphony of fire,
With wild, untainted, puritanical, sexspiritual desire.

Wrath of Odin

There is cold fear in their eyes,
An unusual thing to witness, in these strong and hardy seamen,
Un-settling.

It is so difficult to stand,
My hands are clamped, white-knuckled to the rail,
The Bridge window cavorts from crazy angle, to crazier angle.
There is no vision, just curtain after curtain of rampaging water,
My back aches, pain in my knees and legs from the continual
    struggle to stay upright.

Wave after pounding grey-green wave, rages over Bridge
    window and roof,
Water shouldn't be this high, not this high,
It climbs over us like some monstrous alien,
Battering our meagre fortress, thundering against her shivering
    hull, like blows from Thor's hammer.

She shudders and trembles uncontrollably,
Every weld under incredible strain,
Will she split?

Tons of water pour across her decks amidships and astern,
Heaving her bows skyward, almost breaking her back,
Thirty-six hours without respite, without sleep,
She heels too far, too far,
Will she capsize?
Are we to founder?

Odin, what has angered you so?

Captain gestures his helplessness, his exhaustion, surrenders, a
     man beaten,
Folds like a man kicked, and vomits into the half filled bucket,
Which overturns again, and skitters across the Bridge floor,
Adding underfoot slime to our mounting problems.

I turn my head away, and look to the window, focusing on
     hopelessness.

Below decks, sick men curse and groan, anticipating imminent
     death with every quivering roll, each juddering thump,
     each inpouring rush of cold seawater, our cabins are awash.

I catch fractured glimpses of sky, better unseen,
Black menacing mass, pregnant with evil intent, joined to the
     sea as one, having swallowed the horizon.
Dark ominous fog closes in around us, like Lucifer's cloak,
And worse, much worse, this sea of Death has so many fingers,
Iraqi mines litter these waters, seeking the merest contact.

Rain spears knife us, for daring to poke our puny faces outside,
     to gain vision,
The screaming demonic wind, slices our ears, rips at our eyes,
     and drives a slashing taloned claw, deep into our lungs.

We are sailing into the envelope of Hell,
Praying against God's lick and seal, sending our little vessel, and
     us, post haste to Eternity, with either rending explosion,
     or cold sup of saltwater, a last drink of bitter brine, to cheer
     our departure.

Lightning zaps and crackles all around us,
Making spectral faces of my brave companions,
Strobe-lit blue-skinned dancing corpses, moving like sub-sea
     creatures,
Are we dead men already,
Is this nightmare the curtain veiling Valhalla?
If so, let us pass through swiftly.

I have been, so long, so very long, on, and under these seas,
The sea has fed me,
Paid me,
Nurtured me,
And carried me safe,

Perhaps today,
Is the day she has chosen,
Perhaps today,
She shall cancel all my debts.

(January 1991)

Once

She never spoke to praise him,
Never a smile to raise him,
Never regarded him proudly,
Nor acknowledged his efforts loudly.

Only the decimation,
The cold assassination,
Of every thing he stood for,
She thought him little good for.

Watching love slip fast away,
He wondered would there come a day,
Whilst pondering over the past, she'd say,
'I loved him, once. . .
Before he went astray.'

Feeling

Empty as an oyster shell,
    Discarded, on the shore,
Lonely as a distant star,
    In cold suspension evermore,
Trembling as an autumn leaf,
    Windswept across the park,
Aching as the soulful song,
    of the solo meadowlark.

Wandering as the babbling brook,
    That ambles through the hills,
Colder than the sparrow,
    Left behind to winter chills,
Hopeless as the blinded beggar,
    Tripping through the rain,
Breaking like the young girl's heart,
    Who gave her love in vain.

Wishing for a better day,
    When life proves warm and sweet,
Brittle as the ice that cracks,
    These stones beneath my feet,
Bewildered by the smiling faces,
    Passing, passing by,
Shattered as the stricken tree,
    By lightning from the sky.

Falling as the falling snow,
    That dies at touch of Earth,
As each of us die day by day,
    From the moment of our birth,
Calling out for understanding,
    Calling out for peace,
So disillusioned with this life,
    And longing for release.

Asking all the questions,
                    As to why? and when? and how?
And trying to accept things as they are,
                    At least for now,
Searching for a Haven,
                    Quiet, to sanctify my soul,
And dying deep inside,
                    A wounded spirit, laid so low.

Drifting as the ships that sail,
                    Beyond the seven seas,
Rummaging within my heart,
                    For understanding please,
Gather round me those few friends,
                    Who seem to give a damn,
Hold me in your warmth,
                    And just,
                              Accept me, as I am.

Away

I suppose I should have tried,
To 'ride' the weather,
I suppose I really should have stayed at home.

But then, I left 'cause things aren't getting better,
If a man must be this sad,
He's best alone.

Over ancient lands and foreign seas,
I wander,
The eyes of strangers see a passing stray.

I write these simple words,
To whom succeeds me,
You would not know me,
Hence,
I went away.

Song of Solitude

What bird of exile,
Flutters its wings,
At the inner walls of my heart,

What beast of freedom
Roams the land,
Of my past hopes,

Who can I be,
This cold and solitary stranger,
Adrift upon these alien seas?

I set my course for the stars
And seek oblivion,
At the ends of this Earth,

A silent oarsmen through the clouds,

A song of solitude,
Echoing,
Through the aching soul of humanity.

Seasons

Spring, is the season of beginnings,
Summer is the crest of life's wave,
Autumn, is the death of all reason,
And Winter, is the landscape of lost hope.

What's Left . . . Is . . .

. . .just a tender moment
of compassion,
a fleeting breath,
a single heartbeat of regret,
a murmured word,
a gentle touch,
a cooling ember,
a sign that flutters
in the breeze,
saying
'House to Let'.

no gifted tongue
shall ease the pain
when love has ended,
nor words explain
to those whose lives
are laid to waste,

that errant spirit
in one
changes like a season,

a sign
left swaying
in the soul,
saying,
'Heart to Let'.

Bereaved

Anger is a futile furrow to plough.

The tree shall not speed its growth at my whim,
The mountain shall not lower its peaks,
Nor the sea shallow her depths at my will,

Nor shall time pass more quickly,
Or slow its pace to appease my desires.

Rain shall neither fall nor cease,
The sun neither shine nor fade at my command.

Though grief pierce my heart like a lance,
And turn my blood to ice water in my veins,
Still no jurisdiction have I,
Over this cold, still, silent flesh,
Lying breathless and pale, in Death's strong arms before me.
I can neither command, deliver, nor resurrect,
Though solemn my wish,
And fervent my prayer,
Or sacred, my intent, promise or plea.

I am mortal,
Flesh of this dead flesh,
Clay of this open earth,
Mere man, and vulnerable to this, agony of soul.

Yet, as God is my stern Judge,
I shall continue to face this life,
With all the strength, determination and courage,
I can muster.

I shall continue, with pain as my morning fayre,
And grief as my lonely supper.

I am wounded and laid low,
But forward I must,
Forward I shall,
And, as you would have wished,
Always, as a man,
To the last as a man,

A man, fit to be called,
Your son.

Yesterday's Friend

I cannot conform, to your desires,
Share what we have until it expires,
Drink here your fill,
Consume what you will,
Leave what you spill,
From the protein and the poison of my pen.

Don't quote me mysteries, expecting answers,
Sip from the glass,
Of destiny's chances,
Follow sweet fate where'er she dances,
Keep on learning,
Keep on burning to the end.

Speak not of love,
Late,
When I'm leaving,
Is it I, or yourself,
Whom you are deceiving,
Love me,
And I shall but leave you grieving,
So be strong when I'm gone,
My yesterday's friend.

Blue Eyes

It's all been said before,
About eyes such as yours,

Blue eyes,
Intricate, hard to fathom,
Oceans to cross, horizons, with mystery beyond,
A veil of secrecy.

And I am uncontrollably adrift,
On, strange undulating tides, and irresistible currents,
Vast seas, swirling within the depths,
Of your impenetrable,
Blue eyes,
You've heard it all before,

Blue eyes, harbouring worlds within,
Flash of silver, blink of blue,
And I am snared within a web of woven iris and ebony,

Feeling like an obsessed astonomer,
Entrapped within a cage of, celestial questions,
Looking to immeasurable skies,
Fascinated, intrigued, mystified and forever drawn,
To stars beyond reach, worlds within worlds,
Beyond knowledge, or sweet merciful attainment.

I would wax lyrical and joyfully tell you such things,
But silver tongued eloquence, I fear, is beyond such as I.

Should ever, silence, take those lips,
Should ever those blue eyes, flicker, and close, forever.

Count me damned,
Shut me for eternity, into unresolved Hell.

Instead, whilst we yet live,
Grant me that Promised land, within those blue eyes,
To sail and explore, to search and to find, to love and to learn,
And to languish in the soft soul satisfying Paradise,
Of your, stunning blue eyes.

If only I could muster the courage,
And poetic eloquence,
To tell you, about your, incredible,
Blue eyes.

My Island

I feared that height upon which I trembled,
Subject to the hypnotic pulling power,
Of your eyes, enticing me to fall.

And now having fallen, perilously headlong,
At your wish,
Shall you save me?

Shall you cushion my mouth,
With your sensational lips?
Shall you open your arms in welcome submission,
Snatching me from cruel tides of uncertainty,
To clutch me close, secure against the velocity,
Of my heart wrenching tumble?

Pressing me to my utter, unending joy,
Against the soft yielding warmth of your lushious breasts?

Shall you wrap yourself around me, enfolding me like a womb,
Never to let me go spiralling off, heart over head into emptiness?

Will you be my island?
May I cling to you, with all I have,
Lips locked to your lips,
Thrusting myself unto, and into your moist and delicate body,
My fingers entangled in the wealth of your glorious hair,
Possessing you, arms, legs, lips, hips and heart,
All of you, straining, writhing, pushing and clinging,
To cease my fall, or by our joining, increase it?

So then my love,
Without further hesitation, I have cast myself to carnal chance,
Plunging deliberately into the hot feverish demands,
Of this sea of desire,
We are one,
This pulsation in our blood, waves of wonder,
This throbbing in our hearts, the march of angels,

You, are my island,
In the churning seas of sensation,
You take me in flight, to galaxies unlimited,
Together we spin through the Universe,
Our wanton, quantum leap, through time and space,
Hold tight, my love, my island,
Hold tight.

Lust by Candlelight

Lady in the candlelight,
What secrets do you know,
What does my mind reveal to you,
As you gaze into my soul?

Inviting eyes shine through the gloom,
Lips whispering my name,
The Lady in the candlelight,
Who sets my heart aflame.

Lady of the blue-black hair,
Warm body, hot desire,
Lady of the wild caress,
Who turns my blood to fire.

Lady of the violins,
Sweet Lady of the lute,
Who banishes the lamb in me,
And beckons forth the wolf.

Lady of the sultry skin,
And sensuous the dance,
Sweet Siren of temptation,
Dark Sorceress of chance.

Lady of the smoothest flesh,
Skin like silk or satin,
Lady of the gentle breast,
The world outside forgotten.

Lady, let us die this night,
Love long and lie together,
With no remorse, and no farewells,
Just lust, and lust forever.
Just lust, and lust forever.

141

Look Back Sometime

So what else is there to say?
We've had our love,
Love had its day.

Then,
Mounting its flaming chariot,
Rides off,
Over the hills and far away.

Sad isn't it,
In many ways,
Look back sometimes, won't you,
And think of those early days,
Those you described as ecstasy,
Enthralled, exciting, passion filled nights,
When neither heart, nor head,
Were willing to confess,
That love comes, thrives, thrills.
But never stays.

I was ever enriched,
By the limitlessness of your intellect,
Warmed and mystified,
By the frightening depth and power,
Of your love for me.

Love which I needed,
And used,
And, sadly, abused.

Now,
The short, sharp, shock,
Of realizing I desired it to end,
While it was still fresh,
Unsoiled,
Not, damaged and renewed, ad infinitum,
Damned to inevitable deterioration,

It was love,
It was lovely,
We lived it to the full, then.
Sacrificed it,
While it was still, pure.

Look back sometimes, won't you,
Retain, just a little love, in your heart,
Sadness will keep the memory,
Beautiful.

And so, my young love,
Because I loved you,
I leave you,
Time will ease your tears.

Perhaps, when you are older,
Reflecting in the firelight,
Of some cosy future family nest,
Or through cold years, should you find yourself alone,
This memory will comfort you.

Look back sometimes, won't you,
I shall walk in eternal springtime,
Through the evergreen valleys of your heart,
And smile all your summers, when you seek for me.

Just close your eyes,
And we shall be together,
As we were.

Life shall not dominate us,
Nor the world destroy,
The perfection,
Of all that we once shared.

Age shall not plunder us,
Neither the toil of years,
Nor life's cares,
Shall scar your memory.

No death of joy,
Shall show on our faces,
Only,
The soft,
Gentle love that was,
And our past selves,
Who shared it,
In times of pain, or loneliness, the memory shall come to us,
Like a beautiful old movie,
Happily replayed.

Gathering Dusk

Oh sweet quill of ecstasy,
The poet preens his pen,
When women love what poet writes,
Walks proud among all men.

Rhymed and reasoned, radiant fair,
Caressed, possessed, but slow,
Like satin, comes the silent night,
Relaxed in afterglow.

Opened flower, by whispered word,
Surrendered, gently won,
Sweet perfume of woman's flesh,
When lust's soft deed is done.

Still lingering there, love's fragrant musk,
All through her dreams to weave,
As rising with the gathering dusk,
The poet takes his leave.

Beside Myself

Careful, tread softly,
With extreme caution,
Do not arouse the angry stranger,
Who dwells behind my face,
He is quiet now,
SSHH, let him be.

For when he springs forth,
Suddenly, without warning, like a twisted nerve,
I am stunned, by the sheer force of his hostility,
The violent army of words, lunging ferociously,
Like white heat,
From this stranger's mouth, I am wearing.

Who is this fire blooded, hot tempered aggressor?
Spewed forth like molten lava,
To take control of my emotions, my lips, my voice.

I do not wish to harbour such an entity,
As this trespasser within,
I grapple with him for possession, of my tongue, my actions,
But his anger is fierce, all consuming,
His wrath dreadful, overpowering,

And I cringe at the fear of him,
I have seen,
In other men's eyes.

He is not I, this intruder,
I want no part of him.

I wish only to be gentle and kind,
To live in peace,
I long for warmth, affection, needing only to be loved.

He is not I, this wild warrior,
This battle scarred terror,

Not me,
No part of me,
This stranger,
This appalling stranger.

Cold Picture

Picture years which lie ahead,
Alone amidst the flowers,
Within the gardens of your heart,
Where blossoms empty hours.

Who will understand your pain,
Or the fires within, still burning,
When those you've loved have turned away,
And those you love, are turning.

Death of an Author

He's tiring now, words won't come,
Mourns death of inspiration,
His writing's gone, it won't return,
There is no consolation.

He said it all, laid bare his soul,
And waited while they pondered,
Over tales of broken dreams,
And years of youth, he'd squandered.

And now he sits in silent room,
The typing keys lie muted,
Rejection slips lie all around,
Unopened, undisputed.

The paper packs sit stacked and sealed,
The dust upon them thickens,
His heart's as stagnant as a tomb,
The writer's soul now sickens.

A man must be, but what he is,
And he's been many things,
But the author in him lost the race,
Against time's beating wings.

He sits before the silent keys,
And dreams about the past,
When rhyme and rhythm, poem and prose,
Came pouring forth so fast.

He's nodding now, those tired old eyes,
Are closing in the gloom,
All he seems to do most days,
In his wordless writerless room.

So ancient now, so frail and weak,
His body worn and thin,
His broken heart so feebly beats,
Beneath his mottled skin.

Outside his window, shadows grow,
As night-time cloaks the day,

And as the stars climb high and bright,
The old author, slips away.

The Iceman

Don't expect too much of me, that is deeper than the skin,
I am 'sealed' inside my suit of mail, so pain cannot seep in,
This body is a fortress, standing strong around this heart,
My life is moated waters, that keep the world and I apart.

My eyes reflect no inner thought, my smile reveals no sorrow,
My lips confess not woe nor joy, nor hopes held for tomorrow,
This face contains no misery, there is laughter, there are tears,
Shows no regret, the mould is set, a mask of wasted years.

The little children touch my hand, their innocence will teach me,
That love is locked so tight within, that even they can't reach
    me,
The fallow landscape of this heart, is colder than the snows,
The gardens of this soul contain, no solitary rose.

The mind recoils from love 'that's love' this heart is walled with
    ice,
Yet the body burns with warm desire, responding in a trice,
The eyes of women breathe a flame, across this sallow skin,
The seeds of need sprout strong and fierce, the wary heart, lets
    nothing in.

The body needs, the body bleeds, the body craves relief,
The spirit holds its shield aloft, and hides behind its grief,
These hands are such, the art of touch, is gifted to these fingers,
These lips beware, are skilled and share, an afterglow that
    lingers.

These arms will hold you, warm and safe, caressed, at rest and
    sated,
Soft winds will blow, all through your soul, till the golden glow
    has faded,
And 'love' will whisper through the air, its silver silken wonder,
And 'love's' warm breeze, and deep green seas, shall rise to take
    us under.

Remind yourself of whom I am, a frozen automaton,
And don't believe, or be deceived, suppress all wild elation,
A woman with 'true love' to give, is sacred, none should maim
    her,
Don't dash your heart to pieces on, this sealed and vacant
    chamber.

Come rest your head upon my chest, remembering, all I've told
    you,
Lay your body next to mine, and let these arms enfold you,
And as we linger, mouth to mouth, the fires begin to smoulder,
I beg you, try to reach this heart, which rapidly grows colder.

This 'state' I have described to you, is not a state of choice,
If you can kindle fire 'WITHIN' my being shall rejoice,
'Twould take the sister of the sun, to be equal to the task,
And asking freedom, from this hell, is much too much to ask.

Freedom, from this icelocked hell, is much too much to ask.

Soul to Soul

When my last caress still lingered on your body,
Where my fingers traced your skin, and then withdrew,
When my last kiss left you feeling rather oddly,
Just as though I were still mouth to mouth, with you.
When the sudden chill of dawn came flowing round you,
To fill the space where I'd lay by your side,
And you knew this was the morning I'd be leaving,
You turned towards the wall and softly cried.

When I spoke with futile words of consolation,
Trying hard to lend some comfort to your heart,
You had descended to the depths of desolation,
Though you'd known from the beginning we would part.
I laid my hand so gently on your shoulder,
And tried to speak the words which wouldn't come,
I was struck by how your body had grown colder,
How your tender heart was beating like a drum.

'Twas never meant, that I, should cause you sadness,
For a little while we shared the glow of love,
It meant so much to give and take such gladness,
We blended like a hand within a glove.
If fate had changed the game, to let me stay there,
If destiny, had kept me by your side,
I'd have gone down on my knees in thanks, to pray there,
And how quickly I'd have dried those tears you cried.

Today, I count these distant miles in thousands,
Endless days like wounds, which time won't heal,
And if you're still alone, and share this aching,
Then you'll know right now exactly how I feel.
There is no peace of mind beneath the Heavens,
There is no distraction, deep beneath these seas,
The tides might cease, the stars might fade forever,
But the memory of your tears will never ease.

The winter's in, the nights are chilled and empty,
And wind and storm have struck this small ship sore,
Way overhead a night flight glides to tempt me,
To fly back to your arms forever more.
This world's a lonely place, in mid-December,
And Christmas time just leaves me feeling cold,
I shall remember, and remember, and remember,
Mouth to mouth, heart to heart, and soul to soul,

Mouth to mouth,

Heart to heart,
. . . and soul to soul.

The Ee-Ven-Gel-Lest and the Hypocrite

He calls himself, the EE-VEN-GEL-LEST.
And he quotes the Holy Word,
He twists the whole New Testament,
Till it all becomes warped and absurd.

His choir is a harem of nubile girls,
All short skirts and bobby socks,
And his 'angels' wear satin or shiny suits,

As they pass the collection box,

Oh how the crowd play right into his hands,
All fainting and swooning around,
And the touch of his hands is deliverance to them,
While all I can see is a clown.

He's a flashy cold blooded hypocrite,
A cash grasping son of a bitch,
With a con man's promise of Paradise,
For milking the gullible rich.

How foolish this world with its wealth in the hands,
Of the victims of liar and flirt,
When with neither a penny nor pound they would part,
For the children who die in the dirt.

So he may call himself the EE-VAN-GEL-LEST.
But soul saving isn't his goal,
His only concern is the fortune he earns,
And the cash coming in on the roll.

Those silly old fools think they're buying their way,
Through his doorway to Heaven itself,
But his honey wet lips and his Paradise prose,
Will relieve them of hard earned wealth.

155

And those lovely young girls, all blonde hair and curls,
Tanned legs and eyes all agleam,
When he turns on his charm, Mothers see with alarm,
That this 'celibate's' not what he seems.

He's a rampaging lecher seducing young things,
An ass grabbing son of a bitch,
With a con man's promise of Paradise,
For seducing the gullible rich.

So I'm learning to be an EE-VEN-GEL-LEST.
I've just got to have me some of that,
I've been watching him closely, I know all the tricks,
These people want just what he's got.

So move over there Mister EE-VEN-GEL-LEST.
And leave some of that cream for a brother,
'Cos you know, us ass grabbing EE-VEN-GEL-LESTS
Got to learn to assist one another.

Lend me that mike here, you son of a bitch,
This EE-VEN-GEL-LEST, has something to say,
I can charm the knickers right off a nun,
And brother . . . don't get in my way.

(August 12th 1991)

156

The Observer

'He's cracking up, cracking up!
Look at him, just look,
You see it don't you, don't you see it?
Have you tried to hold a conversation with the man,
Go on, talk to him, try!
I've seen it all before, seen it all before,
It's plain to see, obvious, plain to see,
Just listen to the man, listen,
Are you listening? You're not listening,
If you listen, you'll hear it, you must listen!
He's cracked, cracked and gone, gone I tell you,
Listen to him, listen!
Twice he says everything, everything twice!'

Battle Weary

I am besieged, by an army of days,
An army, reinforced, by weeks, and months, and years.

I slay my enemy, in daily ritual,
I see them die,
And see them die,
And see them die,
In seasons.

Legions,
Their numbers are incalculable,
An invincible force,
And I,
Grow weary,
Grow weary of the battle.

My eyes grow heavy,
And close,
Though I know well,
The danger of careless vigilance,
My arms grow loath,
To parry the blows,
My head sags low, of wounds,

'Time' rallies his regiment.

Scream quietly,
Your war cry, vicious life,

As I,
Shall murmur my death,

Come,
One last warm summer day,
To befriend me,

In sweet restful eternal sleep,
Whisper to me, how it will be,
To feel no more,
To feel no more,
To feel,
No more.

There now . . . I am still,

Cover me with Autumn.

Four Words in Prayer

P   lease,
E   verlasting
A   ll knowing God,
C   ease by thy Holy Hand, the
E   vil that afflicts our land,

i
n

I   ntervene, swiftly,
R   edeem those minds lost to violence,
E   radicate oppression, terror,
L   awlessness, suffering,
A   nger, death and destruction, ease
N   ational disharmony, act with Your
D   ivine Will to save our souls, to save

A   ll
M   en from
E   ternal,
N   emesis.

Wages of Terror

We are a civilized people,
We worship,
We hold our 'god' in highest esteem,
We pay homage,
Make human sacrifice, daily,
Of the old and the innocent,
Upon altars, constructed of bomb blast, bloodied bullet,
And the bones of massacred children.

Nothing stands between our 'god' and us,
Not compassion, nor pity, nor morals, nor any semblance of our
    lost humanity,
We are the disciples of death,
Death to our people,

Brutal, beastial and merciless are our hours of worship,
We are treachery,

Our people, in fear and solitude behind feeble locked doors,
    curse us,
Our souls are damned,
Our 'god' is 'terrorism'
And we are his minions,
Gripped for eternity,
In the taloned fingers,
Of our master, Satan.

The Taker

I,
Am the Taker!

And from you,
I shall take,
Everything!

I know nought of giving,
Of taking,
I know all.

I am the Taker,
First,
I shall take from you,
The womb wherein you lay,
Sheltered,
Warm and soft,

Safe from the world,

You shall be cast out,
Into the world,
A world full, of Takers.

You shall be cosseted, by doting parents,
Wrapped in security, blanketed in love.

But I am the Taker!
And I shall steal from you your infancy,
And hurl you into the agonies of youth.

Where you shall learn,
The imperfections of your parents, their failings,
Their weaknesses,
I shall thrust upon you the knowledge of their fraility,
Their 'Saintlessness'
I shall grind your face in their mere humanity,
And dangle their mortality, under your nose

And when I choose,
I shall obliterate them,
Wipe them off the face of the earth,

For I am the Taker!
And I shall see you squirm,
As you struggle to deal with the pains of reality.

You may strive for love,
And for a while,
I shall tease you with such mortal trivia,
You shall know love,
Taste it, feel it, need it,
Become addicted, dependent.

Then shall I inject the complexities of life,
Dark dangerous doubts,
Vile suspicions, financial stress,

I shall instill havoc,
In your foolish human, petty relationships,
With silken promises of something more,
Something infinitely better, more desirable, more compatible
More beautiful, richer, warmer, wiser.

I shall lure you,
Weaving my intricate web of passion.

Then, like the spider,
I shall watch and wait patiently,
Witnessing all,
As you destroy yourself, and others.

For I am the Taker!

And love is a given thing,
And all that is given,
Shall I take from you.

Learn, if you can,
While your strength remains,
For I am behind you, at your shoulder,
Ahead I lie in wait,
And run as you will,
I shall be beside you,
In possession,
Of the very breath you draw.

Your youth shall be,
The merest moment,
A rustle in the trees,
A sprinkle of falling waters,
A raindrop, hurled from the skies,
And gone forever.

For I am the Taker!
And I shall take from you,
The joy of young blood,
The strength of youth,
The courage of a young heart, as yet undaunted,
Yet enchanted by life,
I shall steal away your confidence,
Take your future,
And turn it mercilessly into your past.

For I am the Taker!
And I shall leave you only,
A pain-wrecked body,
In sagging flesh and crinkled skin.

I shall leave you disillusionment,
Dimmed eyes and trembling hands.

And 'Young' will be, a memory,
A fading photograph, that haunts you.

Your mirror image shall be,
A reflection of all I have robbed you of,
Prepare yourself,
I wait for no man.

For I am the Taker!

You may surround yourself with material treasures,
Your raiment,
May be diamond studded,
Your residence,
A palace of gold,
Structured to stand forever.

You may say,
'Look, at the strength of these golden walls,
Look, at my fabulous wealth,
All is mine, and no one can dispossess me'

But I am the Taker!

And I say 'Fool!'
I shall not take your wealth from you,
I shall take You! from it.
This very day, your life you shall forfeit.

And I shall take from you, your final breath.
Your last heartbeat,
I shall steal the light from your mind.

And as you subside into that awesome darkness,
At last you shall know,
The Universe shall shout my name,

You shall see me for all that I am,
All I have done,
All that I have begun and ended,
All that has gone before you,
All that never came to pass,
You shall learn of my deceit,
My diabolical treachery,
You shall at last perceive,
That precious gift you possessed and wasted.

For I am the Taker!
And my name is 'Time!'
That most prized possession,
And 'Time!' is the greatest Taker! of all.

A Shipyard Yarn

In the drab stillness, of a Belfast morning,
The sun climbs East, and day is dawning,
In terraced houses, men are turning,
Waking, blinking, stretching, yawning.

In their minds a voice is heard,
And half in sleep they hear each word,
An infant ship calls to the herd,
Whose tools are quietly waiting.

She sits encased in a cloak of steel,
And calls the day to turn the wheel,
The 'workers' must be called to heel,
Her oceanic soul's pulsating.

'Build me fast and build me strong,
Ensure my engines can't go wrong,
The sea she sings her beckoning song,
I must soon be underway.

Run me through the final test,
Check my shafts, my welded breast,
Send me slipping from my nest,
Into the salt sea spray.

I am heedless of mere men,
Who brought me life through toil and pain,
Their labours are required again,
My kind must be increased.

Though Belfast was the birth of me,
I'll roam the oceans far and free,
Of all the lands and ports I'll see,
Your Belfast means the least.

So haul them from their cosy beds,
To weave my web of metal threads,
We keep them housed and keep them fed,
My sister ships and me.

And when their working days are done,
Let Ireland's soil reclaim each one,
Bring to the yard each new born son,
Apprenticed there to be.

For ships are more than mortal man,
Since sailing on the seas began,
Unlimited by human span,
Of three score years and ten.

Who cares about their petty lives,
Their scrawny kids, their worn wives,
As long as ships and shipyard thrives,
There'll always be 'the men'.

So bring the tugboats, start the tow,
There are places I must go,
You'll see me passing to and fro,
Somewhere on your horizon.

Your Belfast is beneath my glance,
I'm off to trip my deep sea dance,
My soul so filled with wild romance,
You'll never feast your eyes on.

I am not tied, as you, to tools,
You live and work and die like fools,
Abiding by your shipyard rules,
In poverty and danger.'

But,
As she sailed, the yardmen cursed,
They cursed her sorely, last to first,
And far at sea, her boilers burst,
Now,
The deep seabed has claimed her.

The Misfit

Searching for identity,
Unfamiliar images,
Cluster and converge,
Blend and fade.

Faces smile,
Glare,
Stare,
Don't see me.

Can't seem to find my 'Self'
Am I illusion?
Sense of disbelonging in my own skin.

Whose eyes are these anyway,
Whose hands,
Whose lips,
Whose words,
Whose anger,
Whose compassion?

The blood in these veins,
Is a foreign river,
Coursing through strange land,
And I,
An entity, in alien flesh,

A tree without root,
Twisting and turning on rock without hold,
Confusion is the only certainty,
In a forest of uncertainties.

And no one, is whom I believed them to be,
No one, is whom I believed them to me.

So what direction must I place these feet,
To find my 'Home' in a world off its axis?
In this ludicrous, lopsided, lolling life,
To find my . . . 'Home'.

Where?
Where am I alive?
Is this living, 'THIS?'

Transient, solitary wayfarer, wanderer, etc, etc, etc,
Without destination.
Long lost to Heaven,
A forty-four year journey to 'Nowheresville'
Surviving by circumstance,
Feeding on the human chill,
Stomach sick of life, its lies, and the deadly minefields named,
'Relationships'.

Sadness 'Sucks'.

Pennies in the wishing well,
Eyes closed tight, fingers crossed,
Wishing. . . to deatomize, to chrysalize, metamorphose.
Return to the cocoon womb of Earth,
To breakdown and purify,
Away with this cold stranger,
This numbed relic of someone who 'is' no longer,
Oh Lord, to begin anew,
As fine and delicate and wondrous,
As membrane of butterfly wing,
As wine in perfection,
As unbitten fruit in a new Eden,
As the thoughts of an unborn child.

Whisper sweet seductive words of foreverness,
Death promise me peace,

Reincarnate me from emptiness to eternity,
. . . from agony, to Angel,
. . . from aloneness, to God's love.

Virus From the Stars

. . . And all the world was peace, since mankind was no more,
The sun shone in the skies, and waves rushed to the shore,
The sheep grazed on the hills, the cattle in the fields,
Nature soothed her sores and Earth began to heal.

Winds that cleansed the skies, carried seabirds on the wing,
Bubbling rivers sang, all the joys of coming Spring,
Breezes stirred the trees, and the leafy branches sighed,
Of peace forever more, since mankind had left or died.

Forest floors were rustling with the sounds of tiny feet,
With every new born species to make the woods complete,
Spring rains rejuvenate the loam, and life comes pushing
        through,
As though God's Eden garden plan had all begun anew.

Mountains heaved their mighty peaks aloft towards the blue,
Fruit and flower and blossom showed on every tree that grew,
No pollution in the oceans, no oil stains in the sands,
No toxins in the pure sweet air, and not a trace of man.

From the very core of inner Earth, the purest waters flowed,
Nature spread her bounty wide with every seed she sowed,
Seas they gleamed abundantly with shoals of every kind,
Whilst species, hitherto unknown, evolved within the brine.

The Tropics and the rainforests, developed once again,
Everywhere the Earth required, there fell the blessed rain,
The Arctic and Antarctic, in balance they declined,
And everywhere the Sun probed through, the fertile soil to find.

In the valleys, on the hillsides, in the jungles, on the plains,
All was health and harmony, and peace on Earth now reigned,
Nature healed contentedly, her scarred and wounded crust,
And slowly spread her tentacles, across the desert dust.

From somewhere deep among the stars, to pierce Earth's
   atmosphere,
A gleaming spinning silver disc, across the sky appeared,
Gazing from transparent dome, a pale, white human face,
Descendants of a bygone time, returned from outer space.

Saint or Savage

To leave this world, to fly away,
Among the starry realms to stray,
To live, to live, at peace, at ease,
Midst seven-sistered Pleiades.

To fly aloft where angels sing,
To Heaven on a waxen wing,
To soar unto the sun and thus,
To melt like foolish Icarus.

Permit my ears the Siren's song,
And burst this soul free from its bonds,
To sail, to sail, with Saturn's breeze,
A new born space age Ulysses.

To sup sweet wine, to drink so deep,
Let merry Bacchus haunt my sleep,
To sip the sweet fruit of the vine,
Anaesthetise my fevered mind.

To ride unheeding care or fear,
A fleeting spirit cross the sphere,
Astride unerring Pegasus,
Celestial plains mysterious.

To crash and storm the gates of Hell,
To free the souls who therein dwell,
To tear the evil from my breast,
This Satan might be laid to rest.

Or please some ancient pagan god,
And reap the lust beneath this sod,
Sensation, sex and war my quest,
A savage freed, uncaged, unblessed.

This fevered brain shall burst with fire,
Should fate not quench this fierce desire,
To mingle flesh with passion mighty,
With hot, desirous Aphrodite.

Foul death they brought to man and boy,
Bold Paris and the Whore of Troy,
But oh to be that shrewd young felon,
Who stole the love of lusty Helen.

And then to stand beside brave Hector,
Who shed his blood like Trojan nectar,
Crushed beneath those chariot wheels,
And dragged behind Achillies heels.

Woe man, his history, myths and tales,
Why seek we so for Holy Grails,
Would not this Earth be Paradise,
Had man not crucified the Christ?

To banish war and suffering,
Would this not be the sweetest thing?
To banish with our dying breath,
Insatiable, unfeeling death.

How man is torn 'twixt right and wrong,
Our spirits battling passions strong,
All flesh desiring woman's flesh,
Which once possessed we seek afresh.

What fools to thus live all our days,
In barbarous, warlike, Godless ways,
With peace ignored, sate passions first,
Dismissing Christ, to die accursed.

Man is unique, in all Creation,
Through evolution's reformation,
Yet sanity is raped and ravaged,
Midst struggle betwixt Saint and Savage.

Terrorist

Would it cancel all the ruin and disorder,
If they finally remove the Irish border,
Would it rectify the death and the destruction,
If Ireland has to face a reconstruction?

No, no, the dead would still be dead,
And all the blood that has been bled,
Shall not flow back into still hearts,
Nor mend the bodies blown apart.

Our country may, someday be changed,
'Politically' be rearranged,
But the massacres and murders last forever,
And such deeds shall mark your soul, to leave you never.

Someday we may, from fear at last be freed,
Let us pray that is a day we'll live to see,
But can You face your guilty eyes within a mirror?
Knowing well, you've yet to face the Greatest Terror.

How harshly shall God's Judgement then, be meted,
When the toll is read, of lives You have depleted,
Shall sorrow bow your head when Sentence comes?
That for 'THIS' you fired your gun and placed your bombs.

The Order of the Shadows

There are only 'we' few, here,
I am undisturbed by such company,
Unhindered, as I travel by mode of thought,
Across a terrain of painful years,
That rough and jagged landscape of my 'Self'.

Outside, 'Old World' does his turning,
Chaos reigns,

As 'we' sit, resignedly together,
My 'Self'
'Friend Fire'
And the 'Still Sad Silence'.

Time passes,
Evening settles,
And a fourth welcome companion,
Eases in, to join us,
'Dear Old Darkness' gathers round,
And 'we' move closer to 'the Fire'.

I poke a stick into glowing coals,
Sparks crackle and fly,
Wood ignites,
And a smokey aroma permeates the atmosphere,
Already 'haunted' by the spectres from deep within my 'Self'.

'Fire' grunts his appreciation,
Rearranges himself comfortably,
And returns to the consumption, of his 'hot meal'.

Ah. . . yes,
Sometimes 'we' do tend to forget,
Our other illustrious member,

He cranks his gears, clearing his throat,
Chimes to remind us, his influence is ever present,
'Cranky Old Clock' strikes seven,
And resumes his meticulous subtraction,
Tick, Tock, Tick,
Mercilessly cancelling out, my precious moments of mortality,
Upon this ancient Earth.

Many outsiders try,
To inveigle their way,
Into our little society.

'Cold Wind' blows hard, and howls his wrath,
At closed doors and solid walls,

'Lady Rain' pitter patter, stamps,
Her tiny wet feet, insistently,
Against the slippery slate roof.

And often, 'Brother Fog'
Presses his grey unpleasant face, fatly,
Against unyielding window panes,
But never, gains an entrance.

Nightbirds, screech their curses at us,
And fling themselves frantically, against the barriers,
From light and heat,
They scream black spells and evil portents,
From somewhere out in the deep wild night,
And shiver in the creaking branches, of ghostly trees.

But 'we'
Are,
Unimpressed,
Unafraid,
Uninvadable.

'We' are very exclusive,
My strange companions and I,
Non communicado with the cruel world,
And all its treachery and pain,
Its cold hearts and careless love.

If I must live in austerity,
If I must live alone, and loveless,
These will do,
These few old friends will do,
I know them well,
In these I trust.

Five Amigos are 'we'
My 'Self'
'Friend Fire'
the 'Still Sad Silence'
'Dear Old Darkness'
And 'Cranky Old Clock'.

Comrades of the night,
'We' 'hold out' until dawn,
Brothers at Arms,
United in aloneness,
Compatriots, of,
The Order of the Shadows.

(May 1992)

Angel or Insect?

Something there is,
To learn from the Butterfly.

Was not this, that creature which crawled on his belly?
Squirmed and wriggled, amidst the leaves?
A pestilence, afflicting plants and shrubs?

Have we not seen him?
Black hairy and repulsive, inching his ugly body,
Slowly over branches?

Small difference,
Betwixt he, and the lowly earthworm,
But his ability to climb trees.

Did we not witness,
As he ceased his weary undulating progress,
And formed a cocoon around his hideousness?

To de-atomize within,
Dust to dust.

Look now,
Upon that which emerges,
This wonderous myriad-coloured Butterfly.

Look people,
Beyond what the eyes see,
Do we not perceive, the Hand of God,
Here, in this sunlight,

The re-birth of ugliness, to astounding beauty.

Contemplate the emergence from this chrysalis,
Of the presence of Paradise.

This small caterpillar,
Transfigured, from an object of abhorrence,
To one of awe.

From ashes to ashes to Angel.

Such is God's promise,
For the destiny of man,

Nature proclaims it,
Nature demonstrates it,
God has promised it,
Christ, has died for it,

But man,
Can't
See
It.

Circular Road

Is there sunshine over the Emerald,
Are my gardens in new bloom,
Does the Irish breeze smell fragrant now,
Neath the glow of the April moon?

Are the Rhododendrons blooming,
Are my Conifers strong and tall,
The Magnolia, the Holly, the Maple?
Lord how I loved them all.

The Dahlia and Gladioli,
And the roses, abundant and full,
Camelia and Crocus and Snowdrop,
Where the Willow tree shade's so cool.

Was it all just a dream of a future?
Was it folly, each flower I grew?
Was it not meant for me, neither flower, plant, nor tree,
Nor the children who blossomed there too?

Is there sunshine over the Emerald,
Are my gardens flush with bloom?
Where a stranger walks midst the flowers,
And sleeps in my own bedroom.

Where a stranger stares out from my windows,
And pushes my front door closed,
Where never again shall I enter in,
Or say 'Home' is the Circular Road.

(April 1992)

181